IMAGES OF W

RED ARMY AUXILIARY ARMOURED VEHICLES 1930-1945

RARE PHOTOGRAPHS FROM WARTIME ARCHIVES

ALEXEY TARASOV

Pen & Sword
MILITARY

First published in Great Britain in 2021 by
PEN & SWORD MILITARY
An imprint of Pen & Sword Books Ltd
Yorkshire – Philadelphia

ISBN 978-1-52678-598-5

Typeset by Concept, Huddersfield, West Yorkshire, HD4 5JL.
Printed and bound by CPI Group (UK) Ltd, Croydon, CR0 4YY

Pen & Sword Books Ltd incorporates the Imprints of Aviation, Atlas, Family History, Fiction,
Maritime, Military, Discovery, Politics, History, Archaeology, Select, Wharncliffe Local History,
Wharncliffe True Crime, Military Classics, Wharncliffe Transport, Leo Cooper, The Praetorian Press,
Remember When, White Owl, Seaforth Publishing and Frontline Publishing.

For a complete list of Pen & Sword titles please contact
PEN & SWORD BOOKS LTD
47 Church Street, Barnsley, South Yorkshire, S70 2AS, England
E-mail: enquiries@pen-and-sword.co.uk
Website: www.pen-and-sword.co.uk
or
PEN & SWORD BOOKS
1950 Lawrence Rd, Havertown, PA 19083, USA
E-mail: uspen-and-sword@casematepublishers.com
Website: www.penandswordbooks.com

Contents

List of Tables

The History of Red Army Auxiliary Armoured Vehicles, 1930–1945

Introduction

The period between the two world wars was, perhaps, the most important and dramatic in the history of the Russian armoured forces. The events that happened then shaped the form of the mechanized forces for decades. Some decisions made at that time had a tremendous impact and have continued to affect the development of Russian armoured forces to this day. After almost a decade of stagnation, the Soviet Union relatively quickly succeeded in forced industrialization, equipping the army with modern weapons and developing an advanced doctrine known as the Deep Operation (or Deep Battle). Crucially, new equipment and weapons were created and developed within the framework of this doctrine, and for its furtherance.

The cornerstone of the new doctrine was a powerful mechanized force and its key elements were mechanized corps – formations capable of performing independently as well as in close cooperation with other branches of service [**1**, p. 12]. Consequently, mechanized formations (and the army in general) required a huge amount of auxiliary equipment. The auxiliary armoured vehicles were supposed to provide high autonomy, tactical and operational mobility and great striking power – the key qualities of independent armoured formations. The Deep Operation theory had justified the need for the wide range of armoured vehicles, including infantry and ammunition transporters, engineering tanks and bridge-layers, self-propelled artillery and self-propelled anti-aircraft guns, command and control vehicles, radio tanks, medevacs, and much more.

However, the implementation of the innovative theory did not go as quickly and smoothly as expected by the country's leaders. The process was influenced by a number of important circumstances, both internal and external. Internal factors included overly optimistic assessments of the timing of the transition to the new doctrine and overly ambitious plans for re-equipping the Red Army. These factors could be relatively easily managed or corrected by the army leadership and, more importantly, by the 'fathers' of the Deep Operation theory themselves. But the external factors were another matter. The military leaders were powerless to influence them, but they had a strong impact on the pace of implementation of the Deep Operation theory and, ultimately, on the results. External factors included the quality of military training and education, difficulties with the production of military equipment, and the powerful influence of the internal political struggles, which intensified with the strengthening of Stalin's power.

In 1931 V. Triandafillov and K. Kalinovsky, passionate enthusiasts of tank forces and the founders of the Deep Operation theory, perished in a plane crash. Their deaths had a negative impact on the progress of work on the new doctrine. The search for solutions to the problems that arose during the implementation of the theory required their accumulated experience, knowledge and expertise, but they were gone and there was no one to replace them. By 1934 the number of unresolved problems had begun to slow down significantly the implementation of Deep Operation in the Red Army. During this period the country's leadership began to cool towards the doctrine and its creators. Critics of the theory saw the problems and blamed the theory itself, especially its emphasis on using massive mechanized forces, while external factors were not taken into account.

The next significant factor was the experience obtained during the Spanish Civil War. From 1936 Soviet military thinking radically changed its opinion on the use of armoured forces. The use of tanks in Spain was limited and clearly not all-encompassing, and this came to be regarded by the Soviet military leaders as the most realistic expectation of any future war. This distorted vision of the future of military operations, as well as growing pressure from the leadership of the country and from the Red Army, led to a number of hasty decisions. Typically, they did not solve the accumulated problems, but simply created new ones, which in turn caused confusion among military thinkers and also required solutions. The Red Army entered a period of change, which continued uninterruptedly until 1941.

Moreover, in the period from 1936 to 1940 the 'Great Purge' fell on the army and industry. It is noteworthy that it was the tank forces that were the most affected by the repressions. The entire leadership, from Tukhachevsky himself and the commanders of mechanized corps and brigades, right down to the commanders of tank battalions, were removed or arrested, with many of them subsequently executed. The theory of Deep Operation was now officially recognized as erroneous and the fruit of the activities of 'enemies of the people and wreckers'. The achievements of previous years were gradually abandoned. Many types of auxiliary military vehicles were also recognized as 'unnecessary'. It became extremely unsafe to speak out in support of old ideas, or even to suggest new ones. The Red Army commanders and engineers who retained their posts preferred to adopt a passive position, and simply followed the instructions of their leaders in the hope of 'sitting out' the dangerous time. Initiative in both military industry and the army was suppressed for many years.

In terms of armoured doctrine, by 1940 the Soviet Union had returned to the state achieved by the end of the First World War. According to the new views, tanks were supposed to support the infantry and help break through enemy defences. Deep strikes, envelopments, encirclements and swift actions by independent armoured formations had become things of the past. As a result, the Red Army and its tank troops entered the Second World War in an incomplete state and without a clearly defined doctrine for mechanized troops. A relatively large number of tank types were in service and in production, but the army did not have many other types of auxiliary and military equipment. Ironically enough, exactly those areas emphasized by Triandafillov, Kalinovsky and Tukhachevsky as the most important for modern mobile warfare in the mid-1920s, had been hit the hardest, namely, logistics, engineering, repair and recovery, command and control.

The failures of the first two years of the Great Patriotic War forced the Soviet leadership to seriously limit the production of all types of armoured vehicles except tanks and direct fire self-propelled guns and tank destroyers, and this principle remained intact until the end of the war. During the war Soviet industry produced only one type of reconnaissance armoured vehicle, and insignificant numbers of self-propelled anti-aircraft guns and armoured recovery vehicles were introduced. No ammunition carriers, armoured personnel carriers, engineering and sapper tanks or command armoured vehicles were produced at all. Official permission to convert damaged tanks into tractors was only given in the first half of 1944. Only after the end of the war would the army receive fully fledged repair and recovery vehicles based on tanks. Despite all the efforts of Soviet industry and high command, until the very end of the war with Germany, and even in the campaign against Japan, the Soviet tank forces suffered from insufficient engineering, technical and logistical support.

To a certain degree, the need for auxiliary armoured vehicles was covered by American and British equipment provided under Lend-Lease agreement, but it was always in short supply. However, it should be emphasized that it was Lend-Lease equipment and, in particular, automotive supplies that provided the tank formations of the Red Army with the necessary operational and tactical mobility during offensives which, in a number of cases, led to the success of the operations.

Continuous operations

After the end of the First World War the fate of the armoured forces was not as obvious as it looks with the benefit of hindsight. There was no single opinion on the use of armoured forces, nor on how armoured vehicles would look in the future. However, new ideas, theories and doctrines were abundant. Just as widespread cuts were made to military spending, active discussions on the benefits and flaws of the armoured forces unfolded around the world. On the one hand, supporters of the principle of mechanization saw the enormous potential of the new type of armament, which could radically change the very nature of future wars and return manoeuvrability to the battlefield. The major proponents of such ideas were Great Britain and France, who had gained the most extensive experience with armoured vehicles during the First World War. On the other hand, their opponents believed that technology was secondary to a fighting spirit. They considered tanks to be an auxiliary type of weapon, needed only in rare cases and in limited quantities. Surprisingly, this point of view was prominent in both Germany and the USSR. Both German and Soviet theorists assigned tanks, at best, a secondary role – to destroy enemy fortifications perhaps or directly support the infantry, and in some cases to be used as a weapon of intimidation to reduce enemy morale, which was a very real factor in 1916–1917.

It is worth noting that in the mid-1920s the Soviet military leadership adhered to the view that tanks and armoured vehicles were not a separate branch of the military, so they did not need their own support system or organizational structure. Moreover, tanks were actually regarded as being on a par with auxiliary engineering equipment, such as was used for mine clearance or bridge building. Their main role was to assist the infantry when advancing on fortified enemy positions. In other words, views on the combat use of armoured vehicles had much in common with the ideas that originated during the First World War [**2**, pp. 28–9]. The 'engineering' specialization of tanks brought them under the control of the GVIU – the main military engineering directorate.

Such a point of view, to a certain extent, was understandable, since it was based on the technical characteristics of combat vehicles that the Red Army had at that time, which were slow and cumbersome. However, it was impossible to overlook the fact that armoured vehicles all over the world were changing rapidly. The combat capabilities of armoured forces were growing as tanks became faster and more reliable. All this gave reason to believe that in the future improvements in technology would dramatically change the role of tank forces.

In a few radical cases, tanks were regarded as harmful weapons, and mechanization as a dangerous process that could lead to man losing control over machines and ultimately over the battlefield. By the mid-1920s the military-political leadership was firmly convinced that bourgeois countries were seeking to replace people with soulless but obedient machines in order to prevent the unification of the masses and any subsequent revolution.

Since the development of the Red Army was permeated with politics and ideology, this point of view was shared by many Soviet military thinkers including Frunze and Stalin. Moreover, military theoreticians believed that the Soviet Union should not be afraid of bourgeois technologies, since it had a strength that other armies did not possess – people with true fighting spirit, 'imbued with revolutionary zeal and a sense of unity with each other and the state policy' [**2**, p. 42].

This dominant opinion made it possible to justify the technical lag and, up to a certain point, to ignore the issues of army mechanization. The period from 1919 to 1928 was therefore a time of neglect and abandonment for the Soviet armoured forces. That they survived at all was thanks to the titanic efforts of a handful of enthusiasts and stockpiles of weapons left from the First World War and the Civil War. Despite the obvious stagnation in practical terms, military theory in the Soviet Union developed quite rapidly. As early as 1924 Mikhail Nikolaevich Tukhachevsky published his work *Questions of Higher Command*, which subsequently tremendously affected the development of the theory of mechanized warfare. In this work he introduced the concept of 'continuous operations' for the first time. Tukhachevsky believed that if one operation can be divided into a sequence of separate actions, then according to the same principle a series of operations can be considered within the same framework but at a higher level. Enemy forces would be destroyed not in one general engagement, but as a result of a series of linked sequential actions, which were each elements of one major operation. Tukhachevsky himself explained this idea: 'Consecutively conducted operations constituted, as it were, of dismembered elements of the same operation, but dispersed, due to the enemy's retreat, over a large area' [**3**, pp. 187–9].

Tukhachevsky also emphasized the importance of 'constant pursuit and pressure' to increase disorganization and interrupt the enemy's retreat [**3**, p. 188]. Refusal to pursue, on the contrary, could lead in his opinion to loss of initiative and would allow the enemy time to regroup and prepare a counterstrike. Equally importantly, he high-lighted the key elements of mobile warfare: control and communications, logistics, engineering support and reconnaissance, along with security and defence of the rear area, in which he included air defence.

Despite the fact that Tukhachevsky saw future war as mobile and taking place over a significant area, in his early thinking he did not attach much importance to armoured forces and mechanization. 'Armour' he referred to as a tool to support the 'masses of cavalry', commenting that 'in a mobile war, the independent actions of large masses of cavalry are of great importance' [**3**, p. 191]. Over time, Tukhachevsky's views on the role of mobile forces changed. The emphasis on the 'enormous importance of independent action' by masses of mobile troops would remain, but with the cavalry replaced by mechanized forces.

It should be noted that Tukhachevsky's *Questions of Higher Command* had already included many elements that were consequently used in the development of the theory of Deep Operation. The ideas outlined in this work would largely predetermine views on the combat use of Soviet armoured forces and outline the shape of future offensive operations in 1943–1945.

The Spanish experience

Between 1936 and 1940 armoured forces were used in a significant number of armed conflicts all over the world. The Soviet Union and its military were involved in most of these conflicts, with others closely examined by the intelligence service. Perhaps surprisingly, the dominant factor that emerged from these conflicts to shape Soviet military thinking on the use of tank forces was the experience gained during the Spanish Civil War. Even though the subsequent conflicts on Lake Khasan and at Khalkhin Gol, and even more so the war with Finland, were larger and brought more relevant combat experience, the knowledge gained in Spain held sway almost until the beginning of the Second World War.

One of the key aspects of the Soviet assessment of the actions of tank forces was an excessive concentration on the influence of the technical characteristics of equipment on combat operations. At the same time, factors such as command and planning of operations, the quality of training of the crews, and the conditions in which tank forces were used, etc., were often ignored. For example, Wilhelm Ritter von Thoma, commander of the Condor Legion tank unit (Gruppe Thoma), mentions in his reports that Soviet T26 gun tanks could spot German vehicles at a distance of up to a kilometre; from here, safely out of range, their guns destroyed the thin armour of the small Pz.1 tanks, which were armed only with machine guns. As a result, von Thoma urgently demanded a shipment of tanks armed with guns, or at least armoured cars equipped with guns [**2**, p. 249].

By contrast, von Thoma notes a number of factors that hindered the use of tanks by the Republicans, including the unsuitable terrain, the small number of military vehicles on both sides (which did not allow them to be used in force), and the sheer incompetence of the Republican command, which was not able to make full use of all the technical advantages of the Soviet tanks. As a result, the Soviet tank forces did not make a significant contribution to the outcome of the battles in which they took part. For example, during the fighting for Madrid, the Republicans tried to use tanks on barricaded streets. Deprived of the ability to manoeuvre, the tanks were of little use and by mid-November 1936 the Soviet troops had lost thirteen tanks, four of them beyond recovery [**2**, p. 249].

Following the first two years of the Spanish Civil War, the Germans reached two important conclusions. The first was that small machine-gun tanks were not suitable for modern warfare. The second was that the Spanish experience, in many respects, was characteristic for this particular conflict and it was obtained in extremely specific conditions. For this reason, it should not be used for final conclusions regarding the tactics of using armoured forces, and important strategic decisions should not be made on its basis [**2**, p. 257]. However, the Soviet leadership considered the war in Spain to be a true model of a future war, which should be used as the basis for developing the requirements for new equipment, armaments and, ultimately, the armoured doctrine.

The inadequacy of military equipment was seen as one of the main reasons for the failures. For example, one of the conclusions drawn by military advisers was that Soviet tanks, despite their tactical and technical superiority over German and Italian tanks, were still not suitable for modern warfare. In particular, Rodion Yakovlevich Malinovsky, who served in Spain in 1937–1938, emphasized in his report that 'the reason for the high losses from defensive weapons and artillery during the conflict was the lack of armour protection' [**4**, p. 35]. As a solution, he recommended the replacement of the BT and T-26 tanks with new strongly armoured models. The proposal gave life to another round of modernization of the tanks in service and the start of the development of new models.

In turn, Meretskov and Simonov, in their report to Voroshilov and Shaposhnikov on 5 August 1937, based on the experience of the Spanish Civil War, came to even more controversial conclusions amid large-scale generalizations. In their opinion the actions of tank forces in any future war would inevitably be associated with high losses owing to the development of anti-tank artillery. They believed that in the future tanks would not be used *en masse*, since more tanks on the battlefield would mean more targets, and hence losses would be higher. According to the authors of the report, the rate of annual irrecoverable losses of tanks was supposed to be three to four times greater than the initial number of tanks in the theatre of operations. The authors named artillery preparation fire as a factor that could reduce tank losses, while factors such as the terrain, the duration of the conflict and the correct use of tank forces were ignored by them. The impact of Deep Operation tactics on loss reduction was also not considered [**5**, pp. 234–9].

Ultimately, the Spanish experience became one of the catalysts for major changes in the organizational structure, armaments and doctrine of Soviet armoured forces.

The Story with 'Hangers'

In the mid-1930s the Soviet military leadership began to show dissatisfaction with the course of the army's reorganization, including the rate of implementation of the Deep Operation doctrine. According to the Automotive-Armoured Tank Directorate (ABTU), one of the main problems hampering the introduction of the new doctrine was the poor level of command and control in mechanized formations. Various ideas were put forward to solve the problem. One of the initiatives was a proposal to reduce the number of tanks, remove the auxiliary units in mechanized formations and get rid of 'extra' types of armoured vehicle, including auxiliary types.

It must be emphasized that the Red Army had very little experience in managing large formations such as mechanized corps. The first two corps (the 11th and 45th) were formed in the autumn of 1932 [**6**, p. 107]. By the winter of 1934 they had been in existence for a little more than two years but had taken part in just one exercise, which was held in the Ukrainian Military District (UkrVO). During this exercise, a number of shortcomings were identified. In addition to the usual complaints about the poor interaction between armoured units and other branches of service, mention was made of the inadequate level of command and control, weak mobility and insufficient means to hold occupied territory.

Despite such frankly insufficient experience, I.A. Khalepsky, the head of the ABTU, reached some very serious conclusions. In December 1934, reporting at a meeting of the Military Council under the NKO of the USSR, he noted that 'the organization of the mechanized corps is too cumbersome' because it is overloaded with 'hangers' – as he called the auxiliary units. In his opinion, all these units only complicated the command and control of the mechanized corps and devoured 'a huge amount of gasoline and lubricants' [**7**, pp. 129–92]. According to his rough estimates, auxiliary units required as much fuel and lubricants as 'was needed for two combat tank brigades within the mechanized corps' [**7**, pp. 129–92].

Khalepsky proposed a radical revision of the organizational structure, stating that 'the corps should be left as an operational unit, where the only "hangers" supposed to remain are Headquarters and means of command and control' [**7**, pp. 129–92]. The list of 'hangers' he wanted to get rid of was lengthy and included 'a special chemical battalion, artillery, combat engineers and a bulky reconnaissance battalion that does not meet the requirements of a corps-level mechanized formation' [**7**, pp. 129–92]. Later, in January 1935, he added air defence units to the list of 'superfluous' units, and also offered to re-equip all corps with a single model of tank. He considered the BT to be the best option for the tasks of the mechanized corps [**8**, pp. 21–7]. At the same time, he proposed to increase the striking power of the corps by attaching an assault aviation brigade and replacing the weak rifle brigade with a stronger motorized division [**8**, pp. 21–7].

With regard to mechanized brigades, Khalepsky had a more extensive experience to call upon, as the first experimental mechanized brigade had emerged in 1930 [**6**, p. 106]. Based on a comparative analysis of experiments and manoeuvres, he developed a number of proposals, which he detailed in a report to Voroshilov in January 1935. In his opinion, on the one hand the army could use mechanized brigades in a variety of combat conditions, but on the other hand, regardless of whether the brigades were used separately or as part of a mechanized corps, their current structure was too cumbersome and, as in the case of the corps, required reorganization. Among the main elements that required improvement, he named controllability, mobility, the ability to conduct prolonged combat operations and cross-country ability on all types of terrain [**9**, pp. 17–18].

It should be noted that the proposal sounds quite sensible even today, with a similar set of requirements put forward for modern mechanized formations.

However, despite his sound thinking, Innokenty Andreevich Khalepsky proposed to solve all the problems using a rather strange set of solutions. Firstly, he considered it necessary to continue the course of reducing the number of troops. In his opinion, the number of tanks in each platoon had to be reduced from five to three or four. Secondly, he proposed to drastically reduce the quantity of auxiliary vehicles, including ammunition transporters. Instead, tanks should take on this function and carry all supplies on board. Thirdly, he put forward the idea of replacing some of the armoured cars and heavy tankettes used for reconnaissance with motorcycles. (Looking ahead, it is worth noting that this is exactly how Soviet tankers were forced to perform during the Great Patriotic War, thus giving rise to the rather awkward practice of using combat tanks for every possible function from transporting troops and supplies to towing artillery.) Finally, self-propelled artillery was to be replaced with artillery tanks (a common designation for self-propelled guns on tracked chassis, such as the AT-1, SU-6 or SU-8). Khalepsky does not specify which vehicles should be replaced with what, although there were huge differences between self-propelled guns, both in design and in their tactical role. For example, the AT-1 was an assault gun similar to the German StuG, while the SU-6 and SU-8 were 'classic' indirect fire artillery.

In sum, Khalepsky's proposals turned the mechanized brigade into an almost homogeneous tank formation. The only additional combat arm left in the brigade was motorized infantry. Again, their number should be reduced, and the inevitable drop in firepower was compensated by an increase in the number of machine guns. The issue of the mobility of motorized riflemen was intended to be solved by equipping them with motorcycles or tracked vehicles. But, as in the case of self-propelled artillery, Khalepsky expressed himself very vaguely, without naming specific types of equipment or quantities. He insisted that the main task of the motorized infantry was direct support of the tanks, quite correctly believing that armoured vehicles alone would not be able to act effectively enough, and he emphasized the importance of close interaction between infantry and tanks [**10**, pp. 18–20].

It should be noted that for all the contradictions in the proposals put forward, Khalepsky did not question the need to have large mechanized formations, or the ability of mechanized formations to act independently on an operational level. Indeed, he emphasized his opinion that 'The mechanized brigade as an independent unit and its organization do not raise any doubts. Such an organization is the most valuable tool in the hands of the army command for solving combat missions independently from the main front' [**7**, pp. 129–92].

No matter how worthy Khalepsky's objective was, his proposals clearly lacked thoughtfulness, balance and, more importantly, verification through experimentation. Moreover, his assessments clearly ignored objective factors affecting the combat use of armoured forces, which led to a distortion of the final conclusions. In fact, such factors as the quality of personnel training, along with the commanders' experience, were more relevant than the organizational structure and the amount of equipment, having a greater effect on the controllability of troops and the effectiveness of their actions.

It was naive to expect that the relatively recently established mechanized forces would instantly master the innovative Deep Operation doctrine and learn how to interact with other arms of service, not least because it was an advanced doctrine, demanding and difficult to master. It was even more naive to believe that it would be possible to enhance command and control simply by reducing the number of subordinate units. Inexperienced commanders poorly commanded 'cumbersome' brigades formed before 1935, but they did not cope any better with 'improved' brigades. It wasn't about the organizational structure.

The rationale of certain proposals also raises many questions. For example, replacement of the engineering and artillery assets of the corps with an assault air brigade could hardly be deemed reasonable. Adding a new and demanding branch of service with its own specific requirements clearly would not have strengthened the command and control of the mechanized corps. Given the obvious limitations in the use of aircraft, such as at night or in poor weather conditions, the combat capabilities of the mechanized corps would be also significantly reduced.

Likewise, the recommendation to abandon engineering units is also difficult to explain. Mobility – both operational and tactical – is one of the key features of mechanized formations, and the absence of engineering units deprived them of a significant prop to their mobility. Without such support, minefields, field fortifications or ordinary water barriers could become insurmountable impediments for tanks.

Eventually, the various proposals that had been put forward were examined by Voroshilov and some of them were approved for implementation. By the beginning of February 1934 Yegorov, chief of staff of the Red Army, had sent to the commanders of five military districts an order to start the transition to a new organizational structure, beginning on the 20th of the same month [**11**, pp. 153–4]. Some of Khalepsky's proposals were also accepted, notably the transition to BT tanks, the decrease in the number of tanks in platoons to three, and the exclusion from the organizational structure of those auxiliary units that Khalepsky considered excessive.

The changes had far-reaching and even unexpected consequences. Not everyone in the army agreed with the new organizational changes, and the old factional enmity between the supporters and the opponents of mechanization revived. Many commanders believed that the reforms were intended primarily to weaken mechanized forces and to give the infantry the highest priority.

However, the unification, in the form in which it was implemented, had an even greater negative impact.

Wrong unification

In theory, unification is a useful and effective mechanism. With regard to the armoured forces, unification could help in choosing the optimal number of platforms, thereby reducing the burden on industry and making life easier for the supply and maintenance services. It is quite logical that it is easier to produce, maintain and operate one or two types of tanks rather than twelve or fourteen.

In principle, the idea of unifying armoured vehicles for the Red Army was not new. For example, the 'Tank-Tractor-Automotive-Armoured armaments of the Red Army' system, adopted on 17–18 July 1929, included a tankette, three types of tanks and tractors (small, medium and large) and various types of military and auxiliary equipment based on common chassis [**12**, p. 1]. It was recommended to start theoretical research on a heavy tank, a bridge (engineering) tank and an infantry transporter, with draft designs to be submitted by 1 October 1930. (It is worth mentioning that subsequently all these types of AFVs would be developed and built in numerous variants.) Two variants of self-propelled anti-aircraft systems were to be developed, based on the chassis of a small tank or medium tractor respectively. The former was to be armed with a universal 7.62mm quad machine gun, the latter with a twin-barrelled 37mm anti-aircraft gun mount. The latter SPAAG gun (in Russian ZSU) was to be dual purpose, for both anti-aircraft and anti-tank defence. This idea was clearly drawn from British experiments with the Birch Gun, a self-propelled artillery gun which was developed in 1925 and saw extensive service within the Experimental Mechanized Force. One of the most remarkable features of this weapon was the ability to fire at both ground and air targets.

The same chassis was also to be used for a smoke tank and radio tractor. (The latter was a tank equipped with a powerful radio station, like the Renault TSF, rather than a radio-controlled armoured vehicle.) And finally, the chassis of a small tank was to be used as a basis for both a 76mm self-propelled gun and an infantry transporter [**12**, p. 1], and the reconnaissance tankette chassis as a basis for creating a 37mm self-propelled anti-tank gun. Three types of armoured cars – light, medium and heavy – completed the system.

Obviously, the results look very balanced, even from a modern point of view. It included three weight categories and three base platforms for both wheeled and tracked vehicles. It also addressed the questions of anti-tank and anti-aircraft defence, communications, camouflage and artillery support, with additional issues of heavier 'breakthrough' tanks, infantry transporters and engineering tanks being investigated.

It is noticeable that most of the combat vehicles mentioned were tied in terms of weight and speed to a single small tank chassis, which was logical, since this type was the main tool of the mechanized formations. Heavier machines had narrower tasks, and their operational range was shorter; in addition, maintenance was more difficult and their logistical footprint significantly larger.

Table 1. The system of 'Tank-Tractor-Automotive-Armoured armaments of the Red Army', July 1929 [12].

AFV type	Based on	Tactical Role	Weight	Speed	Armament	Note
Tankette	–	Reconnaissance; surprise assault	Not more than 3.3 tons, desirably 2–2.5 tons	Not less than 60km/h on wheels and 40km/h on tracks	1 × machine gun	'Convertible' drive, wheels/tracks
Anti-tank tankette	Tankette	Anti-tank defence	Not more than 3.3 tons	Not less than 60km/h on wheels and 40km/h on tracks	1 × 37mm gun	'Convertible' drive, wheels/tracks
Small tank	–	Shock weapon of the mechanized formations; breakthrough tank in mobile warfare	Not more than 7–7.5 tons	25–30km/h	1 × 37mm gun and 2 × machine guns	Amphibious capability desirable
'Convertible' small tank	Experimental design recommended. Operational range on wheels: 300km					
Medium tank	–	Breakthrough of the defensive line in mobile and positional warfare	Not more than 15–16 tons	25–30km/h	1 × 45mm gun and 3 × machine guns	–
Heavy tank	Theoretical study of the issue recommended, draft design to be submitted by 1 October 1930					
Light armoured car	Ford-AA	Light reconnaissance vehicle; mobile fire support	Not more than 1.3 tons	80–100km/h on road	2 × machine guns	Unarmoured, with only an armoured shield in front
Light armoured car, gun	Ford-AA	Not specified			1 × 37mm gun	–
Medium armoured car	Ford-AA with rear axle Jumbo or similar	Combat reconnaissance with reconnaissance detachments and armoured formations	Not more than 3.8 tons	50km/h on road	2 × machine guns, one of them with 360-degree traverse arc	–
Heavy armoured car (Autocar)	–	Heavy reconnaissance vehicle, anti-tank capability	Not more than 6 tons	Not less than 50km/h on road	1 × 37mm gun, 1 × machine gun with 360-degree traverse arc and 1 × bow machine gun	Must have two steering positions, at front and rear
Light tractor	–	Transportation of materiel of divisional artillery, personnel and command personnel and all units of motorized artillery	Not more than 3– 3.5 tons	25–30km/h with a trailer	No	Tracked. Trailed load weight 3–3.5 tons

						Tracked
Medium tractor	Maximum standardization with a light tank chassis	Transportation of ARGK guns with weight lower than 7 tons	Approx. 7 tons	Max. 20km/h	No	No
Heavy tractor	–	Transportation of special power ARGK guns and all heavy loads	Approx. 11 tons	15km/h with a trailer	No	Trailed load weight 11–12 tons
76mm SPG	Small tank chassis	Self-propelled gun for mechanized units; preparation fire, preparation and support of tank attacks, anti-tank fire	Not more than 7–7.5 tons	25–30km/h	1 × 76mm gun	–
SPAAG (Machine gun)	Small tank or medium tractor chassis	Air defence of mechanized units on a march and in battle from attack aircraft	7–7.5 tons	25–30km/h	Quad 7.62mm machine gun mount	–
SPAAG (Gun)	Small tank or medium tractor chassis	Air defence of mechanized units on a march and in battle; mobile anti-tank vehicle	7–7.5 tons	25–30km/h	Twin 37mm anti-air gun	–
Bridge-layer (engineering tank)	Theoretical study of the issue recommended, draft design to be submitted by 1 October 1930					
Smoke tank	Small tank or medium tractor chassis	Smokescreen laying	7–7.5 tons	25–30km/h	No	–
Radio tank	Small tank or medium tractor chassis	Communications for large tank formations	7–7.5 tons	20–30km/h	Telegraph and telephone exchange with a range of 250km in stationary position and at least 60km on the move	Allowed to have a second similar vehicle to service the radio station
Troop transporter	Small tank chassis	Theoretical study of the issue recommended, draft design to be submitted by 1 October 1930				

1. Until the development of new medium and small tractors was completed, the Bolshevik and Kommunar tractors would remain in service with the Red Army. Efforts should be made to increase the speed of these tractors, according to the modernization plan [**12**. p. 1 rev].

2. Special development of a new armoured car was deemed impractical; instead it was recommended to work out the issue of maximum unification of the BA armoured cars with the Ford-A, Ford-AA and Autocar truck models already in production [**12**. p. 1 rev].

This approach was supported by the prominent Russian military theorists Konstantin Kalinovsky, Mikhail Tukhachevsky and Vladimir Triandafillov. It should be emphasized that in their opinion each task required its own 'tool', i.e. a separate type of combat or auxiliary vehicle with a specific tactical role and function. Thus, they regarded unification as a purely technical uniformity. Speaking in modern terms, already by the beginning of the 1930s Soviet theoreticians had come close to the idea of equipping mechanized formations with armoured vehicles on a common platform.

Triandafillov himself believed that uniformity was a fundamental principle in the organization of mechanized units. His reasons for this were quite compelling. First, owing to the differences in speed and operational range, tanks were not able to operate effectively at the same pace as slower branches of the armed forces. A deliberate reduction in the mobility of tank formations, for example by 'tying' their speed to the slower speed of infantry or artillery, deprived tank formations of any meaning, since operational and tactical mobility, along with the ability to carry out quick manoeuvres were (and still are) the key characteristics of tank forces.

Secondly, unified tank formations were more efficient in terms of logistics, supply and mobility. It was sensible to equip mechanized units with armoured vehicles on a common chassis, striving to reduce the number of platforms as much as possible, or at least ensuring that they had comparable characteristics. Uniformity in operational and tactical mobility, including cross-country ability, allowed all units of the formation to act as a single whole. The strike core was to consist of light tanks supported by self-propelled artillery and motorized infantry, who followed the tanks in armoured personnel carriers. The infantry units were necessary because tanks on their own could not hold territory, but there should not be so many infantry units as to overwhelm the organizational structure. In such a case, the advantages of the mechanized formation could be seriously weakened.

These basic principles Triandafillov outlined in his report 'On the system of the Tank-Tractor-Automotive-Armoured armaments of the Red Army' of 5 June 1929 [**13**, pp. 5–18 with rev.]. The report eventually became a fundamental document, and many of the author's ideas significantly influenced the further development of the Russian armoured forces.

As can be seen, Kalinovsky and Triandafillov proposed a completely reasonable structure and organization for the armoured forces. It is noticeable that many ideas were borrowed from the British, who in the late 1920s experimented with such formations through the Experimental Mechanized Force (EMF). Learning from the best should never be considered shameful, but quite the opposite, as evidence of maturity in military thinking and readiness to absorb new ideas.

However, there also was an opposite position that was supported by numerous high-ranking officers and Innokenty Khalepsky himself. Supporters of this point of view firmly believed in the need to focus on creating just one type of tank that would be able to perform all tasks on the battlefield, a kind of 'universal tank' that encompassed all possible requirements and qualities.

One of the main arguments in favour of such a general-purpose tank was to reduce the burden on industry, which had experienced serious difficulties with the production of armoured vehicles in the early 1930s. The weakness of Soviet industry in the 1930s was obvious. The tank-building programme of 1929/30 had overwhelmed it, and it was doubtful whether the development and mass production of such a complex combat vehicle was not altogether beyond its capabilities. Tukhachevsky reported on his concerns in a note to Stalin in December 1930 [**14**, pp. 74–9]. Moreover, he insisted that different types of armoured vehicles were needed to perform different tactical tasks. They had to be developed in accordance with individual sets of requirements and possess unique sets of characteristics.

However, the universal tank was only one way of overcoming production-related problems. The second option was to purchase foreign armoured vehicles, technologies and, if possible, even engineers. In the end, the second option was chosen and ironically it was Khalepsky himself who was sent abroad to purchase technologies and armaments. On 30 December 1929 the Soviet commission began its famous 'shopping tour', with plans to visit the USA, Great Britain, France, Germany and Czechoslovakia [**15**, p. 35]. On his return, Khalepsky mostly had not changed his thinking on unification. In 1931 he discussed again the principles of using armoured vehicles and equipping mechanized troops. He and Tukhachevsky exchanged memos, in which they set out their respective views and debated with each other.

Khalepsky had softened his position a little. Now he believed that the army needed one type of tank for each main tactical role. He considered it necessary to have at least three types of tank: reconnaissance, escort and long-range tank. In his opinion, it would be possible to create models of combat vehicles that could perform more than one role, but not all at once [**16**, pp. 14–15]. Despite the fact that the Soviet commander had moved away from the initially unviable idea of a universal tank that would perform all tasks, his general direction of thought remained unchanged. He was convinced that the mechanized forces only needed tanks, and still tried to impose on them non-characteristic functions.

Tukhachevsky, on the other hand, believed that the army needed a separate type of vehicle for each task on the battlefield. To his way of thinking, the army would need at least six different types of armoured vehicles for specific roles: to destroy artillery, to transport infantry, to destroy machine guns, specialized engineering vehicles, supply transporters and radio tanks [**14**, pp. 18–22].

Khalepsky remained loyal to his 'ideals'. As soon as the introduction of the Deep Operation doctrine began to 'slip', and the position of Tukhachevsky and his supporters faltered, he again put forward his version of unification and managed to 'push' its implementation in 1935. It would be wrong to call him the only initiator of the transition to homogeneous tank units, but without any doubt he played a key role in this process.

What happened in the end? Mechanized corps, which had been an operational-level tool, capable of performing tasks on the battlefield independently, even in isolation from allied forces, turned into homogeneous (in terms of technology) but tactically ineffective formations. Simply put, instead of being balanced formations equipped with military vehicles for different purposes, mechanized corps and brigades became formations that simply had many different types of tanks.

It's hard to imagine, but the problem of multiple types of tanks in service arose in the late 1930s. This issue complicated the life of the tank forces in the USSR, and was subsequently inherited by the Russian Federation. On the whole, unbalanced organizational structure, weak support units and lack of some types of combat and auxiliary vehicles became a real problem for armoured forces of the Red Army. The range of interrelated difficulties that it caused became apparent in the early months of the Great Patriotic War and had a significant impact on warfare in general.

Before the war

The period from 1937 to 1940 was one of the most intense and dramatic for the Red Army in general and for mechanized forces in particular. It is important to remember that this period was dominated by several large-scale social, political and economic processes which directly influenced the development of the mechanized forces.

Aside from the Spanish Civil War, in the period between 1936 and 1941 Soviet tank troops participated in the conflicts at Lake Khasan in 1938, Khalkhin Gol in 1939, the Soviet-Finnish War of 1939–1940 and the so-called 'liberation campaign' in Poland in 1939. Despite the fact that all these conflicts were larger and more relevant than events in Spain, the combat experience gained elsewhere was never regarded by Soviet military thinkers with as significance as the lessons learned from the Spanish Civil War experience. Nevertheless, each of these conflicts added new knowledge, contested old ideas and served as a basis and source for new proposals.

As usual, the leadership of the Red Army was inclined to make hasty decisions. From the contradictory and often isolated experiences of 'small wars', excessively bold conclusions were drawn, and these conclusions often served as a basis for suggestions on the reorganization of the tank forces. The changes were frequently implemented on a large scale and often without any prior assessment. Many Soviet theoreticians were still convinced that the difficulties with the military equipment was the main source of their problems, not tactics, crew training or other objective factors. By 1936 the top leadership of the USSR had become disillusioned with the numerous difficulties encountered in equipping the army and implementing the innovative doctrine. This greatly weakened the positions of the supporters of the Deep Operation theory.

Under the influence of the Spanish experience, the vision of future war shifted more and more towards slow and methodical offensive operations, where tanks should move at the speed of the advancing infantry, with their main role restricted to direct infantry support. The principles of the Deep Operation doctrine had been methodically removed from the field regulations. The new, somewhat simplified vision of the use of tank forces was the direct offspring of the battles fought in the First World War or, at best, the Russian Civil War. The Deep Operation doctrine with its rapidly moving and independently operating mechanized formations was replaced with the slow, step-by-step approach, strict top-down command system and subordinate role of the mechanized forces.

As the military leadership began to implement the changes, gradually moving away from the ideas of Triandafillov, Kalinovsky and Tukhachevsky, 'superfluous' auxiliary units and, accordingly, their equipment were gradually removed in order to improve the organizational structure and controllability of the mechanized formations. Consequently, a significant part of the programmes focused on developing auxiliary armoured vehicles was curtailed or postponed. The balance within the organizational structure of the mechanized units was disturbed, but the 'improvements' did not produce the expected results and the level of command and control remained the same, or even worsened.

Finally, in 1937 the 'Great Purge' began. The repression affected the entire military hierarchy, from the very highest to the lowest levels. In the spring of 1937 many Soviet military leaders were convicted and executed, including those who were directly involved in the development and implementation of the Deep Operation theory. Among them were Tukhachevsky himself, Eideman, Kork, Uborevich and others [**18**, pp. 3–81]. Significantly, the armoured forces and the tank-building industry became primary targets and suffered most from the cleansing. The reason for this is fairly obvious. Since Tukhachevsky was the main supporter of mechanization and the Deep Operation theory, everyone who was somehow connected with him fell under suspicion of participating in a 'military-fascist conspiracy', and subsequently they were either executed or sacked.

Over the three-year period from 1937 to 1940 the Automotive-Armoured Tank Directorate (later GABTU) had been headed by four different leaders; three of them were arrested and executed. Innokenty Khalepsky, head of the armoured directorate of the Red Army from 1934 to 1936 and the chief of armaments of the Red Army from 1936 to 1937, was arrested on 13 November 1937 and executed in July 1938. He was subsequently replaced by Gustav Bokis as head of the ABTU, who was arrested on 23 November 1937 and executed on 19 March 1938. Bokis in turn was replaced by Dmitry Pavlov, who zealously started a new cycle of reforms in the armoured forces. In June 1940 Pavlov was replaced by Yakov Fedorenko. Following the defeat of the Western Front led by him, Pavlov was arrested and executed on 22 July 1941.

At lower levels cleansing unfolded on an increasing scale. For example, Ivan Fedko, the commander of the Kiev military district, reported that in the period from June to 20 November 1937 no fewer than 1,984 commanders and officers were dismissed from the units of the Kiev military district. Of these, 861 were arrested as participants in conspiracies, or as spies and wreckers [**19**, pp. 45–61].

In total, in the Kiev Special Military District (KOVO), 90 per cent of corps commanders, 84 per cent of divisional commanders, 100 per cent of fortified area commanders, 50 per cent of brigade commanders, 37 per cent of regimental commanders, 60 per cent of corps chiefs of staff and 40 per cent of divisional chiefs of staff were relieved or arrested, while at the district headquarters the staff changed by 75 per cent [**19**, pp. 45–61].

By 1938 all brigade and corps-level commanders in the mechanized forces had been removed from their positions, with the exception of one brigade commander and several chiefs of staff. Pavlov reported that a similar situation was observed at all levels of command, up to battalion level, where 80 per cent of battalion commanders were also removed from their posts [**20**, p. 31]. And even ABTU (i.e., his own directorate) was staffed only by 73 per cent.

The industry was also disorganized for some time, and to the extent that in the first quarter of 1937 some factories did not produce a single tank from the planned production run and suspended work on prototypes. For example, K.E. Voroshilov commented that Factory No. 174 over five months in 1937 'handed over only seventeen T-26 tanks instead of 400–500 according to the plan; the plant is not ready for the development of the new T-46 tank; the most significant defects of the prototype T-46 have not yet been addressed' [**21**, pp. 678–80]. The managers of the factories were in a state close to panic, and the entire tank-building programme was in jeopardy. Production resumed in the second half of 1937, but even the T-26, T-28 and BT machines, where the teething problems seemed to have been ironed out, experienced difficulties due to the high percentage of manufacturing defects [**21**, pp. 678–80]. All problems were blamed on 'wreckers, Trotskyists and conspirators'. Regardless of the truth or otherwise of such accusations, even an insignificant mistake or even a simple denunciation could become the basis for the removal of a specialist from his post and subsequent arrest.

The Deep Operation doctrine, which had been subjected to sharp and constant criticism since 1935, was officially called incorrect and 'wrecking'. Tukhachevsky and his associates were personally accused of failures in its implementation. Ongoing experiments were halted, and many of the ongoing projects and areas of research were cancelled. An open demonstration of support for Tukhachevsky's ideas became simply unsafe. Many of his associates, in desperate attempts to avoid arrest, were forced to publicly renounce Tukhachevsky and his ideas. In some cases, it took the most grotesque forms. For example, Marshal of the Soviet Union A.I. Egorov, who had been involved with the development of the Deep Operation theory, in 1937 expressed support for Budyonny's idea of the decisive importance of bayonet attacks based on the experience of the war in Spain [2, p. 267].

Events in the USSR quickly attracted attention abroad, and in summer of 1937 the German magazine *Wehrfront* described the situation as follows: 'The highest posts of the military command were again occupied by absolutely reliable heroes of the Civil War and ignorant people. Military qualifications were sacrificed to the politics and security of the Bolshevik system. The post of the executed Marshal Tukhachevsky was taken by the former Chief of the General Staff of the Red Army Yegorov, a colorless personality … even to a remote extent, he cannot replace Tukhachevsky, although along with Shaposhnikov he is undoubtedly the most capable in the military leadership of the Red Army' [22, pp. 7–11].

In general, by the end of the period several problems had emerged that determined the development of the armoured forces of the Red Army. Firstly, the military leadership of the Red Army had lost its advantage over Western military thinking, particularly regarding the unity of views on the role and use of mechanized forces at the highest level of command. This led to a unique combination of chaos and opportunities for building a new system. Since there was nothing immediately at hand to replace the Deep Operation theory, almost anything else could be developed or proposed instead. The old doctrine and most of the developments from the time of Tukhachevsky were recognized as incorrect, but no one knew the new correct path.

From 1936/1937 the mechanized forces of the Red Army entered a period of continuous reforms and changes which often took the form of 'dashing' in different directions. At the same time, changes at the doctrinal level created the need to change the organizational structure of units and formations, tactical and technical requirements for military equipment, and lastly field regulations and the whole system of auto-armoured weapons. Mechanized corps exemplified the degree of 'dashing' and the high level of uncertainty in the leadership of the RKKA.

Initially, mechanized corps were formed in the autumn of 1932 [6, p. 107] and disbanded in the autumn of 1939. This decision was pushed by the head of ABTU, Pavlov, who chose to use the experience of the Spanish Civil War as his guide. In his opinion, the mechanized corps were ineffective since they were not able to make a deep breakthrough into the enemy's rear and operate there. He ruled out the very possibility of 'such a breakthrough of the enemy's front where a bulky tank corps could be used to develop success' [6, p. 109]. However, in June 1940 the People's Commissariat for Defence reviewed the recent actions of the German tank forces on the Western Front, and on Stalin's instructions decided to re-establish the mechanized corps [6, p. 110].

The employment of German armoured forces at the beginning of the Second World War demonstrated their capabilities and showed and the necessity of using large mechanized formations. Moreover, the manner of their employment was in line with the ideas supported by Tukhachevsky and his companions. Surprisingly to some theoreticians, practice had refuted the assumption that auxiliary units and the numerical strength of a given formation could adversely affect controllability.

According to the table of organization and equipment (TO&E), the mechanized corps in 1938 included 560 tanks and 12,710 men. Tank armies, which appeared in the RKKA in 1943, included 430 T-34 and 210 T-70 tanks (a total of 640 tanks) [**23**, p. 198]. In turn, the mechanized corps within the tank army had 15,740 men and the tank corps had 19,334 men [**23**, p. 201].

Secondly, nervousness and uncertainty grew in the army and industry, as any official or industrial difficulty (and, more broadly, almost any action) could become the basis for an accusation of 'sabotage'. The best and safest model of behaviour, therefore, was passivity and unquestioning observance of the instructions of higher command.

Thirdly, the army and industry had lost a significant number of qualified specialists: officers (up to battalion commanders), managers, engineers, experienced workers and employees. There was often no one to replace them, and no time to train new specialists. From that moment on, both the army and the industry were to experience a constant shortage of personnel, which, ultimately, would affect all aspects of their activities.

In doctrinal terms, the Red Army was rapidly dropping back into the end of the First World War. By 1939 the Soviet leadership had returned to the idea that the most rational uses of tank forces would be direct support of the infantry and suppression of enemy points of resistance when breaking through a fortified zone. Deep breakthroughs, enveloping manoeuvres and swift actions by independent tank formations were not considered. In the temporary field manual of the Red Army from 1936 (PU-36), mechanized forces had played a key role in both offensive and defensive operations, as well as being regarded as the primary means of 'organizing a simultaneous attack of the enemy on the entire depth of their battle formation, with the aim of their isolation, complete encirclement and destruction' [**1**, p. 63]. In contrast, the field manual of 1939 named the main task of the tanks as 'direct support of the infantry and paving its way during the offensive' [**24**]. Under certain conditions, tanks were allowed to be used 'for a deeper attack on the enemy's battle formation in order to destroy his artillery, reserves and headquarters', as well as 'for performing independent tasks in large masses together with motorized artillery, motorized infantry and aviation'. However, the tank troops no longer had either their former independence or their former significance. The main combat arm, according to PU-39, was the infantry [**24**].

The lack of a unified system of views and the trend towards simplification of the employment of armoured forces led to distortions in the organizational structure and unbalanced the system of armaments. Simply put, the tank forces now had a dependent supporting role. This, in turn, made it unnecessary (or deprioritized this issue) to equip tank forces with infantry and ammunition transporters, engineer and sapper tanks, armoured recovery vehicles and self-propelled artillery. Formally, this approach facilitated all elements of the organization and development of tank forces, but greatly reduced their combat effectiveness. Unfortunately, such shortcomings were often revealed on the battlefield.

As a result, the Soviet tank forces faced the beginning of the Great Patriotic War in an 'unfinished' form in every possible sense, from doctrine to the development of new vehicles. The disastrous start to the war led to a series of compelled and short-term decisions that further complicated the situation throughout the conflict. The Soviet armoured forces would achieve their final form only after the end of the Second World War.

Chaos in the system

It should not be thought that in the period from 1938 to the first half of 1941 the question of auxiliary vehicles was completely ignored. Some experts fully recognized the problem, suggested options to solve it and regularly raised questions on the development and inclusion of auxiliary equipment into the system of armaments. However, the Soviet military leadership at the highest level still could not reach a consensus on the role and, accordingly, the form of the armoured forces. This led to a situation where controversial and sometimes conflicting decisions were made within a short period of time. Just as industry and the army began to fulfill the instructions of the leadership there would come a new decision, radically changing the direction. This situation can be vividly illustrated with the following example.

In March 1938 Pavlov, the new head of ABTU, came up with a proposal to reduce the number of types of tanks, essentially continuing the course to simplification proposed by Khalepsky. From his point of view, it was enough to leave three main types: the main tank for operations with infantry and cavalry, a powerful artillery tank for fighting the enemy's anti-tank weapons, and a small amphibious tank for capturing river crossings [**2**, pp. 275–6]. The Main Military Council of the Red Army, in general, supported the proposal to reduce the number of types, but did not approve Pavlov's idea. Instead, funding was allocated to create new designs and modernize old ones. In February 1938 there were nine different models of tanks and tankettes in service. Seven more were planned to be added by early 1939. Four of these were modernized old models, but three were brand new [**2**, pp. 274–5].

By December 1938 views on the system of armaments had changed yet again. The document 'A note of the ABTU RKKA on the system of armoured armaments in the third five-year plan' dated 15 December 1938 mentions thirteen tank models divided into four groups, as follows:

- reconnaissance: T-27, T-37 and T-38;
- combined arms tanks: T-26 with 37mm cannon, T-26 with 45mm cannon and T-46;
- operational tanks: BT-2, BT-5, BT-7 and BT-8; and
- breakthrough tanks: T-28, T-29 and T-35 [**25**, pp. 79–81 rev.].

The authors of the document admitted that although a multitude of tank models had been developed and produced over the previous ten years, they were now unequal in tactical and technical characteristics and combat capabilities and 'cause difficulties in military units in the operational-tactical use of materiel' [**25**, pp. 79–81 rev.]. In order to rectify this situation, it was planned to write off or modernize some of the obsolete models.

The document also emphasized that the development of new models dictated the need to 'create high-level mechanized formations up to armoured armies capable of acting independently and performing all tasks both on the battlefield and throughout the operational depth of the modern front'. These units, according to the authors, required 'a secure rear and a reliable recovery service, which sets the task of reducing the number of types of combat vehicles, of which higher mechanized formations should be formed'. The development and production of the 'new models of combat special and auxiliary types of vehicles' were listed as a priority in the tank-building programme [**25**, pp. 79–81 rev.].

These statements are interesting for two reasons. Firstly, they reflected a fairly sober perspective on both the role and form of the armoured forces. It is noticeable that such ideas as independent mechanized formations equipped with large numbers of auxiliary armoured vehicles, fewer models of AFVs in service and a greater level of unification in order to reduce the burden on support units are all close in spirit and substance to the vision of mechanized warfare supported by Tukhachevsky.

Secondly, these views radically contradicted the ongoing policy of the military-political leadership of the USSR. For example, in the month before the publication of the aforementioned document, in November 1938 the Main Military Council decided to disband the mechanized corps. In the new field manual of 1939, the significance and independence of the armoured forces were greatly limited. In light of this, the position adopted by ABTU is hardly understandable: why were they making plans to form 'higher mechanized formations up to armoured armies' but at the same time ordering the mechanized corps to be disbanded? Even the old designation was to be changed – the mechanized troops would be renamed tank troops [**6**, p. 109].

By 1940 yet another system had been adopted. Now it was planned to leave three main types in service with the Red Army: the KV heavy tank, the T-34 medium and the T-40 small amphibious tank. The T-26 would remain as an infantry escort tank, until it could be replaced by a promising SP tank. The fleet of BT-5 and BT-7 tanks was to be upgraded. After the diesel-powered T-34 entered serial production, the production of the diesel BT-7s should have been discontinued. Medium T-28s also remained in the army, but production was discontinued. Amphibious T-37 and T-38 tanks and the heavy T-35 were removed from service, but would remain with the army until they were worn out. BT-2s were to be sent to training units, while T-27 tankettes were to be disassembled and cannibalized for spare parts and the rest handed over for scrap [**26**, pp. 138–45]. In total, not including modifications and deep modernizations, such as the BT-7M, or specialized vehicles, such as chemical tanks, the system included ten tank models. In addition, significant numbers of prototypes – including three variants of the KV, three more T-34s (one of which was modified for anti-aircraft defence), an infantry support tank, an anti-aircraft self-propelled gun and self-propelled artillery with 130mm and 152mm guns – were approved for development in 1940–1941. There was also a plan to develop a family of specialized armoured vehicles based on the T-28 chassis, including a bridge-layer, and mechanical and electromagnetic mine-clearing vehicles with reinforced armour [**26**, pp. 144–5].

In terms of automotive and tractor armament, the system looked as follows. The Voroshilovets, Komintern, ChTZ-65, STZ-5 and Komsomolets tractors remained in service. It was planned to replace the Voroshilovets with a new tractor based on the T-34; the development of that vehicle was included in the plan of experimental works in February 1940 [**27**, p. 28]. The Kominterns and ChTZ-65s were to be substituted with a promising ST-2 tractor (the STZ-5 with its newer diesel-powered modification), and the Komsomolets with a new tractor designed on the T-40 light tank chassis.

The plan further included replacement of the current wheeled vehicle fleet, which was dominated by GAZ-AA and ZIS-5 trucks (Ford Model AA and AutoCar-SA commercial truck variants, which were not particularly suitable for military service). It was intended to replace the existing models with new ones with increased payload capacity and cross-country ability. For example, the 1.5-ton GAZ-AA was to be replaced with the GAZ-63, a 2-ton truck with two driving axles, the 2-ton GAZ-3A with the 3-ton GAZ-33, and the 3-ton ZIS-5 either with a 3-ton truck with two driving axles known as the ZIS-32 or with the standard 5-ton ZIS-15, and so on [**26**, p. 141]. This plan was never fulfilled and at the beginning of the Great Patriotic War the bulk of the truck fleet still consisted of GAZ-AAs (58.6 per cent) and ZIS-5s (40.4 per cent); crucially for the tank units, they included special-purpose vehicles such as mobile workshops, fuel and oil tankers, accumulator charging stations (PZS) and mobile air compressors [**28**, p. 10].

One of the most interesting documents of that period is 'The state of tank armament and the need to create new classes of tanks', which appeared in February

1941. The authors of the document, Engineer Koloev and Military Engineer of the 2nd Rank Vorobyov, analysed the current state of tank armaments and offered their own vision of the employment of armoured forces and proposed a new system of armaments which, in their opinion, met the modern requirements. The authors had come to the conclusion that modern warfare would combine elements of both positional and manoeuvre warfare [**29**, p. 9]. At the same time the development of a universal tank that could meet the tactical requirements of both manoeuvre and positional warfare was impossible. They concluded: 'A universal tank that meets modern tactical requirements cannot be developed with the armour of the same quality or the type of continuous track drive that we have at this time' [**29**, p. 9]. In their opinion, attempts to push tank-building towards the development of a universal tank were harmful and would eventually slow down the supply of the latest military equipment to the Red Army. Koloev and Vorobyov believed the solution lay in establishing the specialization of armoured vehicles based on the 'carefully thought-out classification of AFVs, taking into account all the achievements of modern military technology and the economy of our country' [**29**, p. 11]. They thus rejected the whole movement towards simplification supported by Khalepsky, Pavlov and others, and in fact returned to the ideas of Tukhachevsky, Triandafillov and Kalinovsky of the early 1930s.

Koloev and Vorobyov divided tanks into three classes – heavy, medium and light – and proposed to determine their tactical and technical properties based upon the particular role assigned to them. In addition, they suggested the creation and development of two groups of special-purpose vehicles (combat and auxiliary) derived from the main classes of tanks [**29**, p. 13]. Thus unification was initially included in the system and the need for combat support was taken into account, which is quite remarkable. Auxiliary equipment, according to their views, 'should be engaged in servicing the battle process for the main classes of tanks and infantry. Filling anti-tank ditches, ammunition supply, evacuation of the wounded, recovery of knocked-out vehicles, technical support on the battlefield, etc' [**29**, p. 14].

Among the special-purpose combat tanks, the authors suggested the following types: a tank-fighter ('*tank istrebitel'*) to destroy anti-tank artillery and enemy tanks; a tank for destroying powerful reinforced concrete fortifications; a mountain tank; an infantry transporter; a medical evacuation tank ('*sanitarny tank*'), a variant of the infantry transporter for the evacuation of wounded; a supply tank for front-line resupply of infantry and tanks; a repair and recovery tank to provide technical assistance on the battlefield and evacuate AFVs to the rear; and an engineering tank capable of performing a wide range of functions, from pulling wire obstacles and filling ditches to building bridges and destroying enemy fortifications [**29**, pp. 42–51].

The authors divided battle tanks into three classes, and special purpose tanks into two additional groups that they referred to as 'A' and 'B' [**29**, p. 13]. 'A' included

Table 2. Classification of tanks [**29**, 13–24].

Classification	1st Class	2nd Class	3rd Class
Purpose	Infantry escort tank in a war of manoeuvre.	Breakthrough tank in a war of manoeuvre.	Breakthrough tank in a positional war.
Armour	Light, capable of withstanding all types of anti-tank weapons including 20mm machine guns, up to 45mm.	Medium, capable of withstanding 37–45mm gun fire, up to 75mm.	Heavy, up to 120mm.
Speed	45–60km/h.	25–30km/h.	12–15km/h.
Armament	1 × anti-tank automatic gun (45–47mm) and 1–2 × machine guns.	1 × 45–47mm automatic gun or 76mm gun and 2–3 × machine guns.	1 × 5–6 inch gun, 1 × automatic gun and 2–3 × machine guns.

battle tanks used for special purposes (e.g., anti-tank-gun destroyers, mountain tanks, chemical tanks and tanks used for the destruction of reinforced concrete fortifications), while 'B' included auxiliary vehicles armed with self-defence weapons [**29**, pp. 39–42]. The choice of chassis for some types of specialized vehicles is also quite interesting. For example, the supply tank was proposed to be implemented on the basis of the KV heavy tank, and the troop transport ('*desantny tank*'), ambulance, recovery and engineering tanks on the basis of the experimental heavy tank '100' (*aka* Product 100 or T-100) [**29**, p. 53].

The system proposed by Koloev and Vorobyov, although not devoid of flaws, was still much more logical and more integral than the one that existed at the end of 1940 and the beginning of 1941. In addition, unlike the armoured weapons system adopted in 1940, it took into account the realities of modern warfare and, accordingly, the army's need for auxiliary armoured vehicles.

The authors noted with regret that, despite the high need for auxiliary equipment, 'we had not paid attention to special-purpose tanks. Therefore, we do not have these important and necessary tanks, and the attempts to develop separate special-purpose tanks, like the prototypes of the TR-1, etc., do not withstand any criticism and have mostly thin armour due to the fact that this issue was not sufficiently thought out and we had no experience' [**29**, pp. 51–2]. With regard to the latter, the authors were not quite right, since quite a lot of auxiliary vehicles had been developed in the early 1930s, but all of them were based on the most modern armoured vehicles at that time, such as the BT and T-26. Of course, by 1941 all the armoured vehicles had become heavier, and it is likely that if Kalinovsky or Tukhachevsky had lived to this time, they would also have chosen a heavier and more protected chassis for the auxiliary equipment.

It is obvious that such frequent course changes, the variety of vehicles in development, in service and in production, the continuous reorganizations, and changes in the regulations and organizational structure had dramatically affected the quality of the tank forces of the Red Army. Already lacking qualified and experienced personnel, there was little time and few opportunities for training. In turn, the industry did not have enough resources to meet newer requirements. It did not help that the military and political leadership still lacked a clear understanding of the role of tank forces in a future war, which led to an incorrect setting of priorities. Despite the excessive number of types of tanks in service or in the form of prototypes, the army still lacked many types of auxiliary vehicles and armaments. Some vehicles, the need for which had been recognized in the early 1930s, at best entered service in the second half of the Great Patriotic War, and more often after its end.

For example, a repair and recovery vehicle on a tank chassis – vital for any army with developed mechanized forces – was allowed to be built only on 8 April 1944 by a special order of the State Defence Committee. Moreover, industry was allowed to produce only fifty such vehicles per month, using tanks 'with turrets and weapons unsuitable for repair' [**30**, p. 178]. By that time the order was hopelessly late and was certainly too late to have any significant impact on the state of the repair and recovery units. Throughout the war, it was the norm for the Red Army to use captured vehicles or 'illegal' field modifications instead of specialized auxiliary equipment. 'If a turret was knocked down or penetrated, we would drop the turret and make a tractor out of the tank. For almost the entire war we made tractors ourselves,' recalled Viktor Mikhailovich Kryat [**31**].

Another example is the development of specialized medical vehicles for the evacuation of wounded from the battlefield. The need for an armoured medical vehicle became apparent in the mid-1930s, and in 1937 a prototype based on the GAZ-AAA truck was built at the DRO plant in Vyksa. It was named the BA-22 armoured medical transport vehicle or motorized medical aid station [**32**, p. 336]. The experience of the small wars in the second half of the 1930s further highlighted this problem. In 1940, at a conference at the Kuibyshev Military Medical Academy of the Red Army, a military doctor of the 2nd rank, A.S. Georgievsky, gave a presentation entitled 'First aid and evacuation of the wounded from the battlefield under enemy fire'. In his speech, Georgievsky noted that the conflicts at Khalkhin-Gol and in Finland showed that field medics suffered significant losses and in a number of cases it was possible to evacuate wounded only by using armoured vehicles like FAI armoured cars or tanks. According to Georgievsky, in order to facilitate the evacuation of the wounded from the battlefield under enemy fire, 'it is necessary to adopt special armoured all-terrain medical transporters, allowing this work to be carried out despite enemy fire' [**33**, pp. 24–5].

It is evident that there was an urgent need for medical transporters. To resolve the issue, both wheeled and tracked vehicles were proposed. However, armoured medical vehicles did not enter service during the Great Patriotic War, and it was not until the end of the 1980s that such equipment, based on the BMP-1/2 and BTR-80 chassis, appeared in the Soviet Army.

In conclusion, by the middle of 1941 the tank troops of the Red Army were in a far from complete state and did not have a clearly defined armoured doctrine. The outbreak of the war had made things even worse. Most of the development programmes for both auxiliary vehicles and some types of armaments were interrupted or discontinued, and the industry almost completely switched over to the production of tanks in increasing quantities. The situation was not helped by further changes in the armoured doctrine that were introduced and implemented during the course of the war.

There are two notable features regarding the Red Army during the period 1941–1945. The first is that the problems that had accumulated by June 1941 had not been solved, largely due to incorrect priority setting. The second feature is that the imperfections in the system of armaments directly influenced warfare up to the operational level. This is clearly illustrated in the next section.

All quiet on the South-Western Front, January 1942

By January 1942 the commanders of the armoured forces of the South-Western Front had accumulated solid experience, which was analysed and summarized by Major General of Tank Forces Morgunov, senior battalion commissar Kotenko and head of the operational-combat department of the Automotive-Armoured Tank Forces (ABTV) of the South-Western Front, Lieutenant Colonel Meredikh. The problem of multiple types of tanks in service was still at the top of the list of issues: 'The tank fleet of ABTV South-Western Front consists of a large number of types of tanks, moreover, some of them have undergone all types of repairs a dozen times. There are thirteen types of tanks in service: KV, T-34, BT-60 [probably a mistake in the document; the author meant T-60], BT-2, BT-5, BT-7, BT-7M, T-26 single turret, T-26 twin turret, T-26 flamethrower, T-40, T-38. Of them only the T-34, KV and T-60 are modern' [**34**, p. 33].

This whole 'armoured zoo' was in a deplorable technical condition. Older tanks and spare parts for them had already been discontinued, but modern vehicles had not received spare parts due to the evacuation of the factories ahead of the German advance. 'There are no new aggregates and spare parts at all, and the surplus has not been replenished,' says the document [**34**, 33]]. The commanders of the South-Western Front had to solve the lack of spare parts through their own efforts, as well as by the 'cannibalization' method. They noted that: 'Replenishment of the losses occurs exclusively due to the repair fund of the South-Western Front and the

South-Western Strategic Direction with a very low quality of repair. During the repairs old parts are installed even without major overhauling and restoration' [**34**, 33].

The difficulties with the materiel and logistical support naturally led to problems with the men. Tankers fighting in obsolete vehicles were 'reluctant to take them into battle, which affects the efficiency of using these models of tanks' [**34**, p. 33]. Simply put, the crews were not confident in the reliability of their tanks and preferred not to take risks in battle. Additionally, the authors of the document noted such problems as 'incorrect tactical use of tanks', which may explain the high losses in 1941, which in turn dramatically reduced the general level of proficiency among tankmen. By the beginning of 1942 the bulk of the cadre tankmen (who had trained before the war) were either dead or wounded. The Soviets did not have time to train reinforcements properly, resulting in low levels of proficiency, tactical awareness and skills.

All these factors led to a number of consequences. Firstly, the tanks suffered huge losses both in combat and during marches or at their starting positions. Secondly, a significant number of tanks required major or medium level repairs, which in turn required the evacuation of broken vehicles to factories. The authors concluded that 'a great need for recovery means' was the result [**34**, p. 33]. However, the armoured forces of the South-Western Front also had obvious difficulties with the means of repair and recovery, i.e. their auxiliary equipment. Table 3 details the units supplied with tractors, as of 25 January 1942.

The bulk of the tractors available to the troops of the South-Western Front were ChTZ and STZ models. At the same time, out of seventy-two Voroshilovets heavy tractors assigned to the army recovery units, only five were available. The evacuation of heavy vehicles was therefore carried out by the ChTZ-60/65 tractors, which 'in no way ensures complete recovery and extremely lengthens the [process]' [**34**, p. 37]. Underpowered and slow-moving agricultural tractors, unsurprisingly, could not cope with towing such heavy vehicles as 47-ton KV tanks. Moreover, only sixty-five out of the total of 458 ST-2 and Komintern tractors that were assigned to the troops of the South-Western Front were supposed to be used as standard means of recovery in tank units. Of these, only four were available.

Table 3. Availability of recovery equipment on 25 January 1942.

No.	Model	Number of vehicles	Available	Deficient	% of availability
1	Tractor STZ (light)	1,393	1,099	294	78
2	Tractor ChTZ (heavy)	2,010	949	1,061	47
3	Tractor Voroshilovets	72	5	67	7
4	ST-2 and Komintern tractors	458	65	402	12

In the ideal case, if all units were fully equipped, there should have been a ratio of sixty-five recovery vehicles per 522 tanks or one tractor per eight tanks. But the unfolding war situation was far from ideal and in reality the tank units of the South-Western Front had a ratio of four recovery vehicles per 300 tanks of different types (including broken) as of 31 January 1942 [**34**, p. 37].

The lack of heavy tractors was compensated, again, by the ChTZ-60/65. The commanders of the ABTV of the South-Western Front described them as 'low-powered, with lower tractive power and speed, which does not make it possible to timely evacuate combat vehicles, especially medium and heavy tanks' [**34**, p. 37]. One can only guess how many T-34s and KVs remained on the battlefield or fell into enemy hands simply because there was nothing to evacuate them with. And this does not take into account the complete absence of armoured tractors on tank chassis that would have been capable of operating under enemy fire.

The third consequence follows logically from the first two. 'Although there are many tank brigades,' the authors noted, 'in fact, they are not capable of fighting, since they are not equipped with the materiel required by the tables of organization and equipment. The existing tanks are of poor quality and are not supplied with spare parts' [**34**, p. 33]. The commanders of the ABTV of the South-Western Front admitted some miscalculations in operational planning, and the weak activity of tank brigades and the small impact of their actions in battle. However, they saw the main problems elsewhere. In their opinion, only the KV and T-34 tanks, which 'allowed the possibility of manoeuvre and a powerful strike against enemy fire weapons', were able to conduct effective combat operations. Other models 'did not reach their goals, dotting the battlefield and roads, increasing losses, fuel consumption and the need for recovery means; for example, 10 Tank Brigade (10 TBr) on a march of 60km even before entering the battle lost twenty-nine out of forty-six tanks due to mechanical breakdowns, and only seventeen took part in the battle'. They went on to conclude: 'These reasons reduce the survivability of tank brigades and diminish their combat activity' [**34**, p. 34].

From the point of view of the authors of the document, the tank brigades suffered losses mainly due to the use of outdated tanks of old models. However, this is not entirely true. Tables 4 and 5 show the whole picture.

As the Tables show, older types of tanks provide the bulk of broken-down vehicles, at 54 per cent. This is a consequence of higher wear and tear and a greater shortage of spare parts. At the same time the new T-34s show slightly better results, although out of 110 available tanks 50 per cent required maintenance and major repairs. It should be borne in mind that at the beginning of 1942 the T-34 still suffered from numerous flaws, not to mention the fact that, in the absence of other options for carrying out 'manoeuvres and powerful strikes', the T-34s had been used more frequently than other models.

Table 4. Report on tanks lost in combat and requiring repairs on
31 January 1942 [**34**, p. 36].

Model	Available	Lost in combat (%)	Require maintenance and major repairs (%)	Battle-ready on 31 January 1942 (%)
KV	14	–	4 (30)	10 (70)
T-34	110	11 (10)	55 (50)	44 (40)
BT, T-26, T-38, T-40, T-60	227	40 (17.6)	124 (54)	63 (28.4)

Table 5. State of the tank fleet of the South-Western Front on
31 January 1942 [**34**, p. 36].

Model	Number (according to TOE)	Available, including requiring repair	% available
KV	105	14	13.3
T-34	177	99	50.3
BT	–	48	74*
T-26	–	38	
T-38, T-40	–	5	
T-60	240	96	
Total	522	300	56.5

* For BT, T-26, T-38, T-40 and T-60 tanks the percentage of availability is calculated in relation to the 240 T-60s.

It must be admitted that the commanders of the tank forces of the South-Western Front were being somewhat unfair, damning obsolete tanks as a kind of unambiguous evil. The Germans used plenty of armoured vehicles with similar (or very close) characteristics and operated them quite successfully. The employment of tanks of all models, types and ages was affected by a whole range of negative factors, from weak combat and logistics support to imperfect organizational structure.

To sum up, these were the conclusions that the commanders of the tank forces of the South-Western Front reached. The first and main problem that they felt needed to be resolved was the 'multiple types of tanks' in tank brigades. As can be seen, Khalepsky's ideas didn't withstand the test of combat. Obviously, homogeneous tank formations did not make life easier for the military, rather the opposite. The report's authors recommended that the outdated tanks should be grouped together and the tank brigades equipped with them deployed on secondary directions. 'Tank brigades equipped with modern materiel [KV, T-34, etc.] should be employed on the main directions. Only in this case will tank units be able to act efficiently and counter modern enemy tanks' [**34**, p. 34].

Considering the circumstances, this advice was reasonable. At the very least, it allowed the workload on repairmen and quartermasters to be reduced, and the army would have units with approximately the same set of characteristics in terms of speed, operational range, armament, etc. However, this step would not solve the issue of the imperfections of the organizational structure. In the absence of support units, everything led up to the wasteful practice of using tanks for all combat and support roles, which is exactly what happened. Until the end of the war the situation would not change significantly.

Another group of issues related to combat service and logistic support, principally the repair, recovery and supply of tank units. Firstly, the authors proposed to 'bridge the gap between modern tanks and recovery means, that is, to reinforce tank brigades with recovery companies equipped with the Voroshilovets, Kim and ST-2 tractors' [**34**, p. 34].

Secondly, it was deemed necessary to switch to 'the aggregate method of repairs by means of army units, which is possible only if tank brigades are reinforced with repair and recovery battalions instead of repair companies' [**34**, p. 34].

Thirdly, army and front recovery companies should be 'legalized by including them to the standard organization and maintaining them on a par with other regular units'. And, fourthly, 'it is necessary to subordinate all the repair funds transferred to the South-Western strategic direction (South-Western direction) to the Front command to ensure centralized planning and employment, the same refers to the repair fund' [**34**, p. 35].

In regards to repairing tanks, it was deemed it necessary to create an exchange fund of spare parts. In relation to the existing tank fleet, it should have consisted of 30 per cent engines, 15 per cent gearboxes and 30 per cent side clutches. It can be seen that the listed parts were the most problematic in the T-34 tank. Additionally, there was a need 'to replenish sets of spare parts regularly, fulfilling the requests of the South-Western Front and performing transportation by road and rail' [**34**, p. 35].

One more group of conclusions reached by the command of the South-Western Front concerned a series of issues that were crucial to the very existence of any tank formation, let alone its combat efficiency, and the authors insisted on the need to 'reinforce tank brigades to the established strength' and to 'immediately replenish the tank, automotive and tractor fleet of the Front in accordance with irrecoverable losses' [**34**, p. 35].

It remains to add that the conclusions reached by the commanders of the South-Western Front and the proposed actions in general did coincide with the set of measures that the State Defence Committee began to implement consistently after the start of the war, 'overcoming serious difficulties', as some Soviet authors admitted [**35**, p. 16]. On the other hand, these measures were seriously overdue; for such enormous armoured forces as the Soviet Union had by mid-1941, a system of technical and combat support should have been established long before the start of the Great Patriotic War.

By the middle of 1942 a significant number of PTRBs (Mobile Tank Repair Bases), separate repair and recovery battalions and evacuation detachments had been formed, and by 1943 changes had been made to the organizational structure of the armoured units. Tank regiments and separate tank battalions were bolstered with technical support platoons (VTO); tank brigades received technical support companies (RTO); and each tank army received a separate tank repair battalion (OTRB) and two evacuation companies [**35**, p. 16].

Compared to the general situation in the three years before the war, the conditions for the Soviet armoured forces had gradually improved. However, from 1943 the Red Army switched to offensive operations, in which mobile mechanized formations played a leading role. It soon became apparent that the steps already taken were not sufficient and the technical support system had to be revised again. In general, the tank troops of the Red Army had a tolerably functioning system of technical support by the end of the war, but even then many issues remained unresolved.

There is one more point worth noting. The changes in the organizational structure meant little without concrete action, although it was a step in the right direction and served as an indicator that at the highest level the problem was at least recognized. For example, a repair and recovery company that exists only 'on paper' and is not equipped with the necessary materiel cannot perform its function. But such cases were not exceptional.

In the meantime, problems in the Soviet tank forces were piling up. At the beginning of 1943 the RKKA faced new challenges in the Third Battle of Kharkov, where Soviet tank units were employed in offensive, mobile warfare.

The 3rd Guards Tank Army in the battles for Kharkov, December 1942–March 1943

The actions of the 3rd Guards Tank Army in the winter of 1942/43 provides another good example of how the lack of support and auxiliary units can lead to the failure of an entire operation. At the beginning of the operation the army had 428 tanks of four different types (see Table 6) [**36**, pp. 1–9].

It is worth noting that at the start of the operation the 3rd Guards Tank Army had already participated in combat and, on average, had the following engine wear:

- KV: 50–70 engine hours
- T-34: 90–110 engine hours
- T-60 and T-70: 75–85 engine hours.

After the formation finished unloading at the Buturlinovka-Kalach railway station, the tanks proceeded to the Kantemirovka area. By the time of the offensive, 122 tanks

Table 6. Strength of the tank units of the 3rd Guards Tank Army at the beginning of the battles for Kharkov.

Units / Models	KV	T-34	T-60	T-70	Total
12 Tank Corps	23	98	24	37	182
15 Tank Corps	–	63	22	28	113
179 OTBr.	5	43	16	3	67
173 OTBr.	5	21	21	19	66
Total	33	225	83	87	428

had not arrived, some due to the two echelons being delayed, the rest due to mechanical breakdowns during the march. The broken tanks remained in place and awaited the arrival of repair units.

In turn, the army repair units were among the last units to arrive at the unloading station, on 13–14 January 1943. This meant they could not immediately begin supporting the advancing tank units, since they were busy repairing and recovering the tanks that had broken down on the way from the Buturlinovka-Kalach station to Kantemirovka. At the same time the recovery vehicles themselves were extremely worn out. Army evacuation units had only seven tractors, comprising three ChTZ-65 tractors in 105 Army Recovery Company (105 AER) [**36**, p. 2], one ChTZ-60 tractor in 106 AER and three ChTZ-60 tractors in 105 Disabled Vehicle Collection Post (105 SPAM). In the tank brigades there were no evacuation vehicles at all, with the exception of 97 TBr., which had two ChTZ-60 tractors. All other vehicles were sent to the rear for complete overhaul [**36**, p. 2].

The lack of repair and recovery equipment was partially compensated for by using captured German vehicles. Thanks to this, the Soviet repair and recovery units managed not only to replenish their losses and sustain their activities, but even to increase their effectiveness during the operation. However, this was still not enough, and the repair units could not cope with the increasing numbers of broken and knocked-out tanks, cars and lorries. The Soviet soldiers tried to work as efficiently as possible with the resources at their disposal but it is obvious that by the beginning of the operation the 3rd Guards Tank Army was simply not sufficiently supplied with repair and recovery means, spare parts and transport. This factor subsequently influenced the effectiveness of the actions of the entire tank formation throughout the entire operation.

At the beginning of active hostilities, the burden on the repair units increased dramatically. Apart from routine maintenance of equipment, they had to recover and repair vehicles damaged in combat. In addition, by 1 March 1943 the 3rd Guards Tank Army had been reinforced with 164 T-34 tanks and the preparation of these

Table 7. Availability of materiel in recovery companies per month, January 1943–April 1943 [**36**, pp. 6–7].

Recovery companies	19 Jan. 1943			1 Feb. 1943		
	Tractors	Cars	Trailers	Tractors	Cars	Trailers
105 AER	3	1	2	11	7	8
106 AER	1	3	5	10	8	6
Recovery companies	1 Mar. 1943			Apr. 1943		
	Tractors	Cars	Trailers	Tractors	Cars	Trailers
105 AER	11	7	8	14	7	8
106 AER	1*	5*	2*	16	13	3

* Materiel in 106 AER decreased in March 1943 due to combat losses.

vehicles for battle also fell on the shoulders of army and corps repair units [**36**, p. 3]. The situation was aggravated by the fact that they had to work in difficult winter conditions during active offensive operations. In addition, damaged and broken tanks were scattered over a large area along the army's route, which had covered some 400–500km [**36**, p. 6].

Due to the lack of recovery vehicles it was impossible to tow broken and knocked-out tanks to assembly points. Repair, if it was possible, had to be done in the field. As a result, the already limited repair and recovery units were forced to be constantly on the move and thus could not concentrate their efforts. All this affected the efficiency of their work and the speed with which damaged tanks could be repaired, which was a critical factor for the advancing mechanized formations.

The situation at the end of the battles for Kharkov, on 20 March 1943, is shown in Tables 8, 9 and 10 [**36**, p. 6].

For Soviet troops, the outcome of the operation was disappointing. The German commanders, skilfully employing armoured formations in active defence, managed to stop the Red Army's offensive and subsequently regained control of both Kharkov and Belgorod. It should be noted that both sides were fighting in the same climatic and geographical conditions and despite the Soviets' substantial numerical superiority in both manpower and military equipment, they were not able to benefit from it.

During the course of the operation, all the problems associated with insufficient attention to support and auxiliary units were clearly manifested. The absence or inadequacy of the auxiliary equipment had a greatly detrimental influence. Weak logistics affected both speed and tactical manoeuvrability. The limited resources and capabilities of the repair and recovery units were insufficient to sustain the combat

Table 8. Strength of the tank units at the end of the battles for Kharkov, 20 March 1943.

Model	In service	Repair needed			Irrecoverable losses	
		Maintenance	Medium	Complete	To be written off	Written off
KV	1	–	13	1	3	11
T-34	12	4	107	17	55	242
T-60	–	–	27	3	13	27
T-70	9	–	45	2	5	35
Total	22	4	192	23	76	315

Table 9. Vehicles recovered during the battles for Kharkov [**36**, pp. 7–8].

Recovered	Quantity
Tanks	
KV	7
T-34	93
T-70	33
T-60	27
Pz. IV	1
Pz. III	6
Captured cars and lorries	33
Soviet cars and lorries	45
Armoured personnel carriers*	10
Armoured personnel carriers, cars and lorries, total	88

* Most likely German APCs.

Table 10. Repairs made by army and corps units during the period from 14 January to 25 March 1943

Repair and recovery units	Maintenance	Medium repair	Total
41 ORVB	94	63	157
111 PRB	76	36	112
88 PRB	54	28	82
93 PRB	58	28	86
96 PRB	55	23	78
71 PRB	9	–	9
Total	346	178	524 (+ 899*)

* Repairs made in tank units.

effectiveness of the tank units and they were not able to return damaged tanks quickly to service in conditions of manoeuvre warfare. As a result, even despite their numerical superiority, Soviet mechanized formations quickly lost offensive momentum, tactical manoeuvrability and the ability to deliver telling strikes against the enemy.

The post-battle report written by the headquarters of the 3rd Guards Tank Army noted:

> The withdrawal of the army began after the enemy broke through the front of the 6th Army and moved into the flank and partly the rear of our troops … a shock group was created consisting of 12 and 15 Tank Corps, 6 Guards Cavalry Corps, 184, 111, 219 Rifle Divisions, 138, 206, 265 Guards Artillery Regiments, 288, 368 Light Artillery Regiments, 97 and 315 Guards Mortar Regiments and 319 and 470 Air Defence Fighter Aviation Regiments. After the 350 RD retreated, the group was surrounded by the enemy due to the lack of fuel and ammunition, which slowed down any manoeuvrability and firepower, thus making it impossible to break through the encirclement. The units were basically forced to destroy their equipment and weapons, as a result of which the army lost all the artillery [**37**, pp. 102–3].

The German mechanized forces, on the contrary, demonstrated exactly those qualities that were fundamental to the principles of using large mechanized formations: surprise, speed, breadth of manoeuvre and a high level of interaction between all the elements of the fast-moving formations.

The 2nd Tank Army in the mud, January–February 1944

From the summer of 1941 to the beginning of 1944 Soviet tank forces had accumulated some valuable experience in diverse combat environments. In addition, by the beginning of 1944 the situation on the fronts and in the defence industry had become more stable than a year before. It would seem that there was every opportunity to generalize the experience gained and to use it as a basis to make the necessary changes in order to avoid old mistakes in the employment of tank forces. However, subsequent events showed that improvements were only partial and in general the situation with the auxiliary units was still far from acceptable. A number of aspects of organization, equipment and support of mobile forces remained problematic, with the roots of the problems stretching back to the chaos of the late 1930s.

The combat performance of the 2nd Tank Army (2TA) in the winter of 1944 may serve as an example of how unresolved issues could affect the capabilities of the tank formation and even jeopardize the outcome of the whole operation. It should be noted that the offensive operations conducted during the winter of 1944 in Western Ukraine were considerably affected by unusually warm weather. On 20 January 1944

2TA concentrated in the area of Belaya Tserkov, where it was replenished with combat vehicles to its full strength [**38**, p. 401].

'Report on the combat operations of the 2nd TA' emphasizes the factor of the weather. 'The operation carried out by the army on 26.1 to 26.2.44 is not similar to any of the previous operations … The distinctive feature of the operation was that it had to be carried out facing absolutely horrific road conditions. There was even a moment when the tanks might have been left without fuel and ammunition' [**39**, p. 361]. The weather affected the performance of the whole army, but logistic support suffered most of all: 'The season did not promise anything good. Warming began at the end of January. Motor vehicles were restricted to highways. Traffic on even country roads was difficult. Nevertheless, the heroic efforts of soldiers and officers contributed to the success of the operation' [**39**, p. 361].

The impact of the weather was aggravated with an unexpected change in command plans. During detraining, the army received an order to redeploy to a new area of operation at Svinamy (Sinarna) state farm [**40**], Lipovets station, Oratov [**39**, p. 361]. From an organizational point of view, this resulted in 'non-simultaneous deployment of formations completely under-equipped with materiel', which made it impossible to use the tank forces in strength and with the necessary support. The report noted that 'Tank formations in most cases entered the battle without fire support, which led to unnecessary losses' [**39**, p. 361].

From a technical point of view, the redeployment meant that routine maintenance of the AFVs had to be performed on the march and at the new positions [**38**, p. 401]. It must be borne in mind that the army had just received reinforcements, and the new materiel had to be thoroughly checked and adjusted. The production quality of armoured vehicles in 1944 still left much to be desired, and the 'freshness' of an armoured vehicle was no guarantee of reliability. Another report written by the Directorate of armoured supply and repair on the combat performance of 2TA emphasized the fact that the order for redeployment was received during the 'unloading and receiving of military equipment' [**38**, p. 401]. In other words, due to haste, some vehicles went to the front with malfunctions of varying severity or without proper checks, which subsequently affected the combat capability of the units.

The muddy roads also affected cooperation between units and different arms of service. The first consequence, which manifested itself almost immediately, was the difference in speed and cross-country ability between wheeled and tracked vehicles. And since 2TA did not have indirect-fire self-propelled artillery, all the artillery had to be towed by cars or tractors, apart from the Guards mortar units (multiple rocket launchers, the well-known 'Katyushas'), which were truck-borne. Thus Soviet tank units were often deprived of much-needed fire support. In addition, 2TA was under-equipped with trucks: out of an established strength of 3,123 trucks, it had only 1,369 (44 per cent) in serviceable condition [**41**, p. 7].

A second consequence was the emergence of confusion due to changes in plans on the fly: 'While everything was static, things were going well, but in the dynamics of the battle everything fell apart. Hasty deployment, and the lack of time to organize interaction according to the plan, led to isolated and uncoordinated actions by army units. Hurriedness in organizing offensive actions, excluding the minimum required time for reconnaissance and surveying, was the main drawback of the army's combat operations' [**39**, p. 361].

This was an unflattering description for a tank army. In accordance with the words of the document's authors – the commander of 2TA, Major General A. Radzievsky, a member of the military council; Major General of the tank forces P. Latyshev; and the chief of staff of the army, Colonel Bazanov – it appeared that 'mobile' tank forces could operate well as long as everything was static and going according to plan.

The third consequence, highlighted by the 2TA commanders, was the frequent resubordination of army units and frequent changes of tasks [**39**, p. 361]. This resulted in tank formations being employed piecemeal, scattered and often even isolated from one another, instead of en masse as powerful shock 'fists'. This not only went against all military and pre-war regulations and recommendations, but also further complicated the already difficult process of controlling a tank army in conditions of manoeuvre warfare.

Even before the start of the operation repair and recovery units were urgently transferred to the army's battle formations. They were tasked to support advancing formations and repair equipment broken on the march or damaged in combat [**38**, p. 401]. However, instead of this, the tractors of the recovery units were engaged in rescuing trucks from the mud on the route from Belaya Tserkov to Sinarna state farm, Lipovets station. According to the reports, the logistics situation was so desperate that 2TA experienced interruptions in supplies of fuel, lubricants, food and ammunition [**38**, p. 401]. Eventually, with the help of army recovery units, the supply was restored, 'ensuring the advancement of up to 1,000 vehicles with various equipment and weapons to battle formations' [**38**, p. 402]. However, it should be emphasized that at the moment when the repair and recovery units were helping the trucks, they were not fulfilling their direct duties – the technical support of tank units.

In addition, the equipment of the repair and recovery units had not changed at all in comparison with previous years: with the exception of low-speed tractors, these were the same 'A' and 'B' type mobile workshops based on the GAZ-AA and GAZ-AAA chassis and, less often, on ZIS- 5 or ZIS-6 chassis, which got stuck in the mud just like all the other wheeled vehicles. A way out of the situation, however, was found. Separate repair brigades with hand tools were sent to the battle formations on foot or directly on tanks [**38**, p. 405]. This solution allowed for repair and maintenance, albeit to a very limited extent. It was not perfect, but still it was better than nothing.

Since the supply of spare parts was also limited due to the awful road conditions, all repairs relied on the 'cannibalization' of broken and destroyed tanks and self-propelled guns. The report gracefully calls it the 'removal of necessary parts and assemblies from tanks written off as irrecoverable losses'. Note that in this aspect 2TA in 1944 was no different from the armoured forces of the Southwestern Front in 1941–1942 [**38**, p. 405]. Considering that there was nowhere to wait for help, and the work had to be done, the repairmen looked for solutions on their own. Specifically, they used tanks that required major repairs as tractors, sometimes installing industrial tools and machinery (cranes, winches, etc.), as well as learning 'to remove gearboxes from the tanks without hoists' [**38**, p. 405]. In fact, in January–February 1944 Soviet soldiers independently made armoured recovery vehicles for themselves, which, as noted earlier, were only officially allowed to be built two months later, from 8 April 1944, at a rate of fifty per month.

Another significant factor that influenced the overall effectiveness of 2TA was the 'abnormal' use of tanks. The repairmen could facilitate their work by adapting damaged tanks with 'field modifications', but other branches of the armed forces did not have such opportunities. In the absence of tracked or half-tracked transporters, armoured personnel carriers, artillery tractors, armoured reconnaissance vehicles and similar equipment, all these functions fell on the 'shoulders' of the T-34s. Two important points are noted in the 'Report of the Department of Armoured Supply and Repair on the Combat Operations of 2TA'. Firstly, 'the number of breakdowns caused by technical reasons amounted to 64 combat vehicles, or 9.7 per cent of the total number of AFV breakdowns' [**38**, p. 404]. Secondly, the failure of the T-34 tanks due to technical malfunctions 'should be attributed not to the poor quality of the vehicle [design flaws], but to the extremely large overload of the tanks, which was caused by off-road conditions. The tanks were carrying sub-machine gunners, stocks of ammunition, fuel and lubricants in barrels, often simultaneously towing loaded trucks' [**38**, p. 407].

In other words, 10 per cent of the combat vehicles of 2TA did not go into battle because they were working as tractors and armoured personnel carriers, until they were out of order. It can be assumed that some of the combat vehicles involved in the same activities wore out and consumed their motor hours faster, which subsequently also led to the failure of tanks and self-propelled guns. The following tables show the data on the losses and recovery of 2TA combat vehicles for the period from 27 January to 24 February 1944.

As shown in the Table 11, from 21 January to 15 February the number of armoured vehicles in 2TA 'dried up' by about six times. By 18 February, due to the attached tank brigades, the number returned to 27 per cent of the original strength and remained at about 30 per cent until the very end of the operation.

Table 11. Changes in combat strength of 2TA, 21 January–25 February 1944 [**39**, pp. 359–60].

Model	21 Jan. (before the operation)	30 Jan.	15 Feb.	18 Feb.*	21 Feb.	25 Feb.
T-34	264	197	58	81	54	63
MK-9**	31	26	–	–	–	7
KV-85	–	–	–	19	29	27
SU-76	12	9	–	–	–	2
SU-85	31	1	1	–	5	10
SU-152	21	8	–	–	16	–
Total	359	241	59	100	104	109

* New tank brigades were attached.
** The Russian designation for the Valentine IX.

Table 12. Number of combat vehicles broken down due to malfunctions, damaged in combat and irrecoverable losses [**38**, p. 403].

Model	Maintenance	Medium repairs	Major repairs	Irrecoverable losses
T-34	140	163	45	152
KV-85	14	16	3	–
MK-9	10	6	1	3
SU-152	9	4	10	2
SU-85	17	17	–	21
SU-76	19	6	–	1
Total	209	212	59	179

Table 13. Number of repairs made by army repair and recovery units [**38**, p. 403].

Model	Maintenance	Medium repairs	Total
T-34	132	128	250
KV-85	14	11	25
MK-9	8	3	11
SU-152	9	4	13
SU-85	17	16	33
SU-76	10	4	14
Total	190	166	356

In total, during the battle 2TA irrevocably lost 179 tanks of all types, to which should be added the 59 tanks and self-propelled guns requiring major repairs, since it was impossible to patch-up them in the field. Out of 209 tanks requiring maintenance, 190 received it. With regard to medium repair, the situation was somewhat worse: out of 212 tanks, only 166 were repaired [**38**, p. 406]. The overwhelming majority of losses were caused by enemy artillery fire. This accounted for 560 combat vehicles, or 82 per cent of all losses during the operation [**38**, p. 404].

Unfortunately, the documents do not contain detailed data on all types of armoured vehicles, which might have given a more comprehensive picture of how the wear and tear on armoured fighting vehicles affected the effectiveness of their deployment. Such data, however, are available for self-propelled artillery regiments, and based on them it can be assumed that this impact was extremely significant. As can be seen from the data given earlier, since mid-January there had been no SU-152s in combat, and by the end of the operation only two had returned to front-line units.

The other report emphasized that, out of the sixty-four combat vehicles that were out of order for technical reasons, six self-propelled SU-152 guns broke down due to significant engine wear [**38**, p. 404]. The combat report of 2TA gave further details about the use of self-propelled artillery: 'Making long marches (up to 300km) led to a high consumption of engine hours and the failure of SPGs. After the first 120km of the march, 17 SU-152s did not arrive on time. After the second march to the Stanislavchik area, 9 SU-152s, 8 SU-85s and 6 SU-76s were out of order and became completely unusable' [**39**, pp. 356–7].

At the beginning of the operation 2TA included twenty-two SU-152s, thirty-two SU-85s and twenty SU-76s. The data given above indicate that as of 25 January there were twelve SU-152s, thirty-one SU-85s and twenty-one SU-76s in combat. Almost half of the SU-152s had already fallen behind on the march. (Different numbers in the same document may have arisen due to the fact that the clerk confused the types of vehicles or the headquarters received incorrect data.) Four days later, on 30 January, only nine SU-152s, one SU-85 and eight SU-76s went into combat [**39**, p. 360]. The main reasons for the drop-outs were mechanical failures of self-propelled guns caused by high consumption of engine hours and poor training of the drivers [**39**, p. 357].

Another document is no less helpful. In the 'Note on the availability and technical state of self-propelled artillery in 2TA' it is claimed that as of 19 February 1944, 1542 Self-Propelled Artillery Regiment (1542 SAP) had all its ten SPGs undergoing major repairs; in turn 1441 SAP out of sixteen SU-85s in total had only four in service condition; the rest were awaiting repairs. Four SPGs were written off as irrecoverable losses [**42**, p. 76].

This leads to the rather unpleasant conclusion that most of the tank army's self-propelled artillery was destroyed by long marches, lack of proper technical support and insufficient training of tankers. The bulk of the self-propelled artillery simply did not reach the enemy, although these combat vehicles were exactly what the Soviet Army needed on the battlefield. The commander of 2TA noted that 'heavily armed enemy tanks and self-propelled guns could be effectively opposed only with the SU-85 and SU-152, which were insufficient to conduct high-intensity battles' [**39**, p. 364]. Thus, without the proper and sufficient technical support, the armament that was most effective against the enemy's armoured vehicles floundered in the mud or stood on the side of the road. The SU-85 self-propelled guns were generally admitted as 'the main and almost the only means of fighting Tiger tanks and Ferdinand self-propelled guns' [**39**, p. 364]. Other armaments turned out to be ineffective against the enemy tanks. The combat report of 2TA also noted that 'during the battle, tank duels had happened. The outcome was negative for us, since the T-34's 76mm gun could penetrate the armour of the Tiger and Panther tanks only from short distances (500–600m), while our tanks were engaged with large-calibre guns from a distance of 1.5–2.5km' [**39**, p. 364]. The effectiveness of the SU-76 self-propelled guns was also assessed negatively. The vehicles were characterized as having 'weak suspension, weak armour-piercing capability and weak armour, thus they show little efficiency in the anti-tank role' [**39**, p. 364].

Lastly, the Guards mortars and artillery simply did not have time to get to the positions in time to join the battle:

> The task of concentrating artillery in the Korsun-Shevchenkovsky area was not completed on time. The main reasons for this were the absolute lack of roads and the lack of an adequate number of transport vehicles. As a result, by 10 February 1944 the firing positions were occupied only with self-propelled regiments and separate batteries, even separate guns. The rest of the materiel was on the way and arrived in the area of action only at the end of combat engagements [**39**, p. 357].

As can be seen from these examples, 2TA did not meet one of the fundamental principles of the organization of mechanized formations. The elements of the tank army had different operational and tactical mobility, which is why they moved at different speeds and could not concentrate their efforts or support one another. This would happen again, largely due to the lack of the necessary auxiliary units and equipment.

The 6th Guards Tank Army in the Manchurian operation, August–September 1945

The last conflict of the Second World War in which large mechanized formations were used was the Soviet-Japanese War. The aim of the Manchurian operation – Operation August Storm in the West – was to seize a number of regions of China,

Korea and Manchuria, defeat the Kwantung Army and, as a result, force Japan to withdraw from the war and subsequently surrender. According to the Soviet plan, the main strike was to be delivered by the forces of three combined-arms armies (39th, 53rd and 17th) and the 6th Guards Tank Army. The latter was to strike around the Khalun-Arshan fortified region from the south in the direction of Changchun [**43**, p. 6].

The main strikes all converged towards the centre of Manchuria, their purpose to quickly envelop the main forces of the Kwantung Army, deprive them of their supply lines, cut the connections with the metropolis and the forces in North China, and then dissect and destroy the Japanese piecemeal [**44**, p. 64].

The idea of the entire campaign was built, to a large extent, on the use of mobile mechanized formations, offering an element of surprise to the strike [**43**, p. 6]. Since one of the key elements of the entire operation was the rapid advance of a large tank formation, it was necessary to pay the most serious attention to maintaining operational effectiveness in difficult terrain, away from their supply lines and in the face of strong enemy opposition. The most important components of the success of the tank forces in general, and 6 Guards TA in particular, thus became logistic, engineering and technical support. It should be noted that by the beginning of the operation on 9 August 1945 the war against Germany had long ended and the Soviet troops, in general, had had enough time for comprehensive preparation, even taking into account the fact that some formations were redeployed to the Far East from Western Europe.

Since the largest armoured formation that took part in the operation was 6 Guards TA, the aspects of that army's logistics, supply, technical support and air defence will be closely examined and discussed. That is to say, those aspects where auxiliary vehicles should have provided invaluable assistance. (Engineering support will be reviewed in the next section.)

The 6th Guards Tank Army consisted of the 5th Guards Tank Corps, two mechanized corps (9th, 7th), two motorized rifle divisions (36th, 57th), one anti-aircraft artillery brigade, four tank battalions, two self-propelled artillery brigades (208th, 231st SABR), two light artillery brigades, two artillery regiments of the RGK, and one motorized engineering brigade, as well as a separate hydro company, one motorcycle regiment and the 57th Regiment of M-13 Guards mortars [**43**, pp. 2, 11]. By the beginning of the operation the army had 810 tanks (800 according to other sources), 193 SU-100 and 26 SU-76 self-propelled guns, up to 359 guns and mortars of all calibres, 129 anti-aircraft guns, 201 mortars and 46 multiple rocket launchers (Guards mortars) [**43**, p. 3]. In general, the technical condition of the armoured vehicles was assessed as good. Of the 1,019 vehicles in total, only 38 required repair, but almost all of them were obsolete BT-5, BT-7 or T-26 tanks [**45**, p. 47].

Table 14. Tanks and self-propelled artillery of the 6th Guards Tank Army before the Manchurian operation [**45**, p. 47].

Unit	M4-A2	T-34	SU-100	SU-76	BT-5, 7	T-26	Total
5 Guards TK	–	208	21	–	–	–	229
9 Guards MK	183	–	23	–	90	–	296
57 MSD	–	–	–	13	–	11	24
7 MK	–	184	21	–	87	–	292
36 MSD	–	–	–	13	–	11	24
208 SABr	–	2	63	–	–	–	65
231 SABr	–	2	63	–	–	–	65
4 GMTsFP	–	10	–	–	–	–	10
4 GPS	–	3	–	–	–	–	3
38 ORO	–	3	–	–	–	–	3
248 ZTB	2	4	2	–	–	–	8
Total	185	416	193	26	177	22	1,019

The numbers of armoured vehicles in the army and the tasks assigned to the tankers obliged the commanders to pay special attention to preparation, especially given the difficult climatic and geographical conditions in the zone of operations, as well as the significant number of outdated tanks within the formation. However, both of these problems were known even before the start of the battle. The top priority issues, therefore, were technical support, repair and recovery.

The documents of the repair units indicate that the BT-5, BT-7 and T-26 tanks produced in 1935–1936 had high engine wear with up to 700 engine hours and significant wear of the chassis and other parts. Moreover, there were no spare parts for these tanks [**45**, p. 48]. Given the nature of the terrain, as well as the leading role of the tank army in the upcoming operation, the decision to include old and worn-out vehicles in the formations looks strange and difficult to explain. In total, older model tanks accounted for 19.5 per cent of the total number of tanks and self-propelled guns of 6 Guards TA. Most of the vehicles of this type had not withstood the difficulties of the long marches and eventually broke down and did not take part in combat, since they were left without fuel and lubricants on the march [**45**, p. 49]. Their role, in fact, was limited to burdening supply and recovery units.

The 6th Guards Tank Army was supported by the following repair and recovery units. At the front level it was bolstered with 125 Separate Tank Repair Battalion (OTRB) and 68 Recovery and Transport Company; at the army level with 49 OTRB, 88 and 138 AER, 145 SPAM and warehouse BTI No. 3214 (a warehouse of armoured equipment); and at the corps level with the 86th, 547th and 549th ATRBs in the 5th Guards TK, 7 MK and 9 Guards MK, respectively [**45**, p. 48].

One positive change in comparison with the period of the Great Patriotic War was the equipping of repair and recovery units with tractors based on the T-34 tank, sometimes referred to as 'T-34 armoured personnel carriers'. The report on the march conducted by the 5th Guards Tank Corps even mentions a tank with a crane. This was most likely a field modification of the tractor based on the T-34 chassis [**46**, p. 192].

The army and corps repair units were fully staffed with equipment and personnel, but the two recovery companies (88th, 138th) each had only six armoured recovery vehicles instead of fifteen [**45**, p. 48]. The units equipped with wheeled auxiliary vehicles and special-purpose vehicles on wheeled chassis remained at the same level, with the number of vehicles even slightly reduced.

As stockpiling began for the operation it became clear that there was a shortage of cars. During the preparatory stage it was necessary to transport all the fuel and lubricants that would be required (a total volume of more than 7,000 tons), as well as sixty-seven wagons of ammunition and all food. The total volume of cargo to be transported exceeded 15,500 tons. In addition, it was necessary to bring firewood and a supply of water. Replenishing water for personnel and vehicles required 472 cubic metres and about 100 vehicles were required to transport it [**47**, p. 9].

The combat report of 6 Guards TA emphasized that 'for the timely concentration of the necessary reserves, the army needed to be reinforced with an auto regiment, allocating one battalion for transporting fuel and lubricants' [**47**, p. 10]. But some units of 6 Guards TA were themselves not fully equipped with automotive transport. The total shortage was estimated at about 2,000 trucks. In addition, the bulk of the automotive transport fleet in the various units of 6 Guards TA was extremely worn. As noted in the report, 'The main difficulty in material and technical support was not lack of supplies, but their delivery to the troops and a deficiency of transport vehicles' [**47**, p. 12]. The automotive transport fleet consisted of a bizarre mixture of vehicles, obtained in different ways and produced in different countries. The reports of the 7th Mechanized Corps are quite indicative and, in principle, illustrate the general supply of trucks, cars and special-purpose vehicles in the entire tank army (Table 15).

It is noteworthy that the bulk of the vehicles in the fleet were either obtained under Lend-Lease or captured. The figures also show an obvious fact: as of 7 June 1945 the 7th MK was underequipped with motor transport by 21.3 per cent. Without the captured and Lend-Lease vehicles, the mechanized corps would have had only 156 vehicles of all types available (effectively 91.1 per cent underequipped). In effect, as a mechanized corps it would have been unfit for action.

Furthermore, 7 MK, like the entire tank army, was insufficiently equipped with auxiliary vehicles. For example, the majority of its off-road vehicles, all its self-propelled M17 anti-aircraft guns and all its half-tracked M3A1 armoured personnel carriers were of American production. (Just as in 1943–1945, halftracks were

Table 15. Automotive transport of 7th Mechanized Corps on 7 June 1945 [**48**, p. 171].

Category	Vehicle		Established strength	Available on 7 June 1945
Light cars	M-1		38	1
	Willys		35	75
	Captured		–	10
		Total	73	86
Trucks and lorries	Truck GAZ-AA		891	18
	Truck ZIS-5		614	39
	Truck Dodge 1.5 litre		–	4
	Truck Ford 6		–	95
	Truck Chevrolet		–	400
	Truck Studebaker		–	322
	Truck Dodge 3.4 litre		–	9
	Vehicles captured		–	258
		Total	1,505	1,145
Special-purpose	Mobile workshop type 'A'		37	26
	Mobile workshop type 'B'		16	12
	Mobile accumulator charging stations, PZS		12	9
	Fuel tanker ZIS-5		37	26
	Medical GAZ-AA		46	20
	Other special-purpose GAZ-AA		20	3
	Other special-purpose ZIS-5		6	2
	Other special-purpose Studebaker		8	1
	Other special-purpose Dodge 3.4 litre		–	39
	Vehicles captured		–	17
		Total	182	155
		TOTAL	1,760	1,386

attached to reconnaissance units.) The situation, as of 30 September 1945, was that 7MK had only fifty-three M3A1 armoured personnel carriers and fifteen M17 Multiple Gun Motor Carriages, of which twenty-nine and twelve respectively were in a serviceable condition [**48**, pp. 169–70]. There were no specialized ammunition transporters, armoured personnel carriers or tractors for artillery systems. Anti-aircraft and large-calibre guns were mainly towed by trucks, thus were dependent on wheeled vehicles. As in the above example of 2TA in the winter of 1944, tanks took over the transportation of some of the infantry and cargo.

Sergei Loza, a participant in the Manchzhur operation, recalled in his memoirs: 'The first tank battalion was reinforced by a company of tank *desant*, who were attached by five or six men per *emcha*.' [**49**] ('Emcha' was the nickname of the M4 tank, derived from the Russian 'em chetire'.) This method of transportation was not comfortable for the troopers and led to sunstroke or injuries, but there were no better options. Subsequently, wheeled vehicles fell behind the tanks due to difficult road conditions or lack of fuel.

Some of the elements of the operational planning were based on pure assumptions. The first was that fuel and lubricants could be replenished by capturing enemy fuel depots. However, this did not happen: 'Fuel was absent throughout the entire route of the army's advance, and only after reaching the Mukden-Changchun region did the army receive several dozen tons of fuel and lubricants' [**47**, p. 5]. (Obviously, this assumption had arisen from the experience of the war in Western Europe, but given the difficult climatic and geographical conditions, the length of the supply routes and the absence of railways, it was a bold move to build a plan of operation for the tank army on the assumption.)

Another assumption was that the repair units could supply themselves with spare parts and assemblies by removing them from armoured vehicles knocked out or destroyed in combat. Since the tank army did not meet any serious resistance, this also failed. The 'Report on the technical support of combat operations of the 6th Guards TA' stated that 'the absence of combat losses excluded any possibility of obtaining spare parts from tanks' [**45**, p. 51].

During the course of the operation, technical support problems became closely intertwined with engineering support and supply problems. In fact, a vicious circle emerged: there were not enough engineering units to build roads and bridges; armoured vehicles, moving through difficult terrain, consumed more fuel than expected and broke down more often; repair and recovery units, also few in number, could not cope with the growing workload; and the supply of fuel, lubricants and spare parts was disrupted due to all these factors combined: stretched lines of communications, difficult terrain and the lack of motor transport. The terrain was a major factor: steep slopes, difficult soils (sand, salt marshes, etc.), high temperatures and dust led to frequent breakdowns of tanks, self-propelled guns and trucks. In addition, the vehicles were forced to move in lower gears, thus increasing fuel consumption. According to the reports, the excessive consumption of fuel on certain parts of the route reached 100 per cent [**45**, p. 51].

Interruptions in the supply of fuel and lubricants to both combat vehicles and repair and recovery units led to the situation in which 'tanks stood idle longer than the allotted time for servicing and resting crews, and the evacuation facilities could not fully use their production capabilities'. For the same reasons, the timely delivery of spare parts and repair units was hampered [**45**, p. 49].

An additional negative factor influencing the actions of the army was the high percentage of new crews. The documents of the 5th Guards Tank Corps state that 'before the start of the march, the corps had up to 70 per cent of new crews with a relatively low degree of training both in driving and in general knowledge of the materiel' [**46**, p. 194]. The decision to staff the units with new tankers looks very controversial, since in the spring and summer of 1945 the army definitely had enough battle-hardened and highly experienced personnel. No less perplexing was the decision to leave experienced crews on outdated combat vehicles, and not to retrain them for new types. These same questions were asked by Dmitry Fedorovich Loza, a Soviet tanker who participated in the operation. In his memoirs, he recalled this episode:

> I still cannot forget the tragedy of the experienced crews of these worn-out vehicles. We 'Westerners' [Loza served on the M4A2 Sherman] were very worried, seeing how they froze one after another in the hot sands of the Gobi Desert, on the first kilometres of a narrow mountain road on the outskirts of the Big Khingan ridge. The tank officers cried without shame.
>
> It was absolutely incomprehensible to us then, and now I ask myself the question: 'Didn't the Far Eastern Military District and Moscow know about the technical state of the tank units equipped with the T-26 and BT?' … 'Why weren't these units re-equipped with new materiel? Experienced cadre officers and their trained subordinates were quite capable of mastering T-34s in three or four months, but they were simply framed [**48**].

The decision to staff tank units with insufficiently trained and inexperienced crews eventually affected the performance of the whole tank army and led to a number of negative consequences, namely, excessive fuel consumption, frequent mechanical breakdowns and uneven movement of convoys. In addition, due to the actions of inexperienced drivers, thick dust was raised, which reduced visibility, clogged filters and impaired the performance of air cleaners [**46**, p. 194]. The last factor is mentioned as one of the most important reasons for the failure of T-34 tanks [**45**, p. 49].

Air defence is a separate and important factor. Equipping such a large formation as a tank army with mobile air defence assets should have a special priority when planning a large-scale operation. Weather, climatic and geographic conditions make this issue even more important. The zone of operations of the 6th Guards Tank Army included numerous narrow and impassable places, where enemy aircraft in relatively small numbers could cause serious damage or even delay the advance.

As mentioned previously, there were few self-propelled anti-aircraft guns in the tank army. But, according to the plans of the commanders, the main cover for the advancing units was to be provided by aviation and towed anti-aircraft artillery. The latter struggled with three particular problems. Firstly, the air defence units were underequipped in terms of motor transport. On average, the anti-aircraft units of the 6th Guards Tank Army had 56.7 per cent of the required number of vehicles, and the vehicles they did have were distributed unevenly. For example, 542 OZAD (separate anti-aircraft artillery battalion) had 93 per cent of its required transport, while all the units of 30 Anti-Aircraft Artillery Division had only 25–30 per cent of the required number of vehicles [**50**, p. 192].

Secondly, the available vehicles of the anti-aircraft units were already worn out and unsuitable for transporting part of the artillery systems. This situation remained exactly the same at the beginning of the operation, forcing anti-aircraft artillery units to simply leave part of the artillery systems in the rear [**50**, p. 192].

The third problem concerned the trucks. All the air defence units of the 6th Guards Tank Army had been equipped with GAZ-AA and ZIS-5 trucks, which, even in perfect mechanical condition, were not suitable for operations in the difficult geographic and climatic conditions of Mongolia and North China. At the beginning of the operation worn-out vehicles began to break down and, as a result, some of the anti-aircraft artillery had to be left behind.

In addition, the mobility of the anti-aircraft units was affected by disruptions in fuel supply and the usual problems with communication. Since the air defence units were equipped with low-power radio stations, the anti-aircraft units often lost contact with the tank units that they were supposed to cover [**50**, p. 193]. It is also noteworthy that, after the army began to experience a shortage of fuel and lubricants, the commanders made the decision 'to supply fuel to anti-aircraft artillery units, like all other artillery units of the army, in the last turn. This resulted in air defence units lingering behind the advancing tanks' [**50**, p. 192]. Thus, due to the lack of motor transport, part of the anti-aircraft artillery remained in the assembly area, some fell behind along the way, and the rest suffered from lack of fuel and had only intermittent communication with the tank units. In essence, the anti-aircraft units and tankers were saved only by the weak activity of the Japanese air force. For example, by 31 August 1945 air defence units had recorded only five attacks by enemy aircraft, one of which was shot down [**50**, p. 193].

A word on engineering support

One of the most important issues closely related to the use of tank forces is engineering support. At the turn of the 1920/1930s this issue rapidly became decisive, and the main catalysts of the process were the development of the theory of Deep Operations and the active development of mechanized troops in the Red Army. According to the new theory, armoured formations were supposed to break through the enemy's defence and further develop the offensive to the entire operational depth. One of the key points of this scheme was speed. Both the breakthrough and the offensive should not have 'stalled' due to the inability to overcome the enemy's engineering obstacles or to quickly cross water obstacles.

One obvious and well-known decision after the First World War was the creation of special engineering vehicles based on tank chassis. Tukhachevsky, in his work *New*

Questions of War, written in 1931–1932 [**51**, p. 62], emphasized the need to create special military engineering vehicles, specifically mentioning 'high-speed sapper tanks capable of overcoming artificial obstacles and quickly removing barriers without crews leaving the tanks' [**52**, p. 186]. Further, he suggested the need for 'new tank-sapper means' which, in conjunction with amphibious tanks, would 'solve the issue of river crossings and many other sapper works in a new way' [**52**, p. 192].

Engineers and industry reacted quickly enough and by in the early 1930s experimental work had begun on the development of engineering and sapper vehicles based on T-26 and BT tanks. By 1934 some prototypes had already been embodied in metal, tested and began to enter service in small quantities.

Nikolai Nikolayevich Petin, a former officer of the Russian Imperial Army and head of the engineering department of the Red Army, produced a report in December 1934 that positively assessed the ongoing changes and noted a serious improvement in the technical equipment of the engineering troops, both in comparison with the Imperial Army and with the Red Army in 1930. In his opinion, the level of mechanization of the engineering troops had grown, and new models of equipment had gradually begun to appear in the army. Remarkably enough, in 1934 the RKKA had sapper tanks, though Petin noted that 'only 50 of them were produced' [**53**, pp. 389–94]. However, neither the number of these sapper tanks nor their characteristics pleased him. 'The sapper tank cannot satisfy us,' emphasizes Petin. 'Now the task is to design a sapper tank to overcome 8m wide trenches, not 6.5m as we have now' [**53**, pp. 389–94].

By 1933/1934 the state of the engineering support in the Red Army had been significantly enhanced and there was a clear trend towards further improvement. The equipment was being perfected in accordance with the requirements of the military and, crucially, was being developed within the framework of a single doctrine for use with mechanized forces.

The introduction of the theory of Deep Operations became one of the key reasons for the modernization of the engineering troops in the Red Army. 'If we turn to the Instruction on Deep Battle, we can see what tremendous tasks are now being set for the engineering troops,' said Petin. However, he soberly assessed the situation and understood that, despite all the positive developments, the mechanization of engineering troops was still at the very beginning of the journey. 'It's all about the lack of transport and tractors,' he noted during one speech. 'We have sawmill equipment, but we cannot use it. We have power tools, but we have nothing to move the compressor stations with, no tractors, no cars' [**53**, pp. 389–94].

It should be noted that without the influence of Tukhachevsky's ideas and his theory, the Soviet military leadership simply would not have seen the need to create a number of engineering vehicles and equipment. For example, the heavy pontoon park N2P was developed and put into service in 1932 and was intended to equip mechanized formations. It replaced the obsolete pontoon park of the Tomilovsky system, developed back in 1868 and adopted by the engineering troops in 1872. Subsequently, the N2P pontoon parks were heavily modernized twice, in late 1941 and early 1945, and served through the entire war. The more advanced heavy pontoon parks (TMP) had been produced in insignificant numbers due to the lack of metal. During the entire war only ten sets were made [**54**].

After Tukhachevsky and his associates were accused of conspiracy, the principles of Deep Operation were gradually abandoned and some of the experimental pro- grammes were curtailed. However, it cannot be said that the mechanization of the engineering troops was completely forgotten. Part of the work was continued, creating in particular experimental vehicles such as the sapper high-speed tank (SBT) based on the BT-2 chassis and the bridge-layer based on the T-26 tank chassis. Experimental engineering tanks were tested in combat conditions during conflicts on the Karelian Isthmus in 1939, but were not adopted for service [**32**, pp. 222–5].

The war with Finland emphasized the importance of engineering support for the mechanized forces, especially when breaking through the enemy's defensive zone in difficult natural conditions. The development of new vehicles was reactivated in 1940.

On 20 May 1941 Fedorenko, the head of the Automotive-Armoured Tank Direc- torate, produced a report entitled 'New questions of struggle' in which he mentioned a rather interesting range of special engineering equipment. Special vehicles intended for overcoming obstacles included the IT-28 engineering tank based on the T-28 tank, a self-propelled bridge on the Stalinets-2 tractor, a mine roller and devices for dropping fascines and explosive charges from tanks [**55**, pp. 22–3].

The first two vehicles had an equal tactical role and were intended to build bridges over horizontal obstacles, such as ditches, scarps and counter-scarps. In addition, the IT-28 could build a bridge to overcome vertical obstacles up to 4.5m high. The length of the track bridge for both vehicles was 13m, with a carrying capacity of 55 tons [**55**, pp. 22–3]. Apart from the presence of armour protection, the main difference between the IT-28 and the bridge on the Stalinets-2 tractor was that the engineering tank had a high degree of automation, transported the bridge on its own and could lay it down without the crew leaving the tank. In contrast, the bridge on the Stalinets-2 tractor was transported on two single-axle trailers and laid by using a swing arm with a winch. This version was not intended for use in combat conditions.

Mine clearance versions and devices for dropping fascines and explosive charges were developed for new models of tanks, the T-50, T-34 and KV. By the end of May 1941 they were at various stages of design. It is known that in 1941 it was planned to order the first batch of fifty-five IT-28 tanks. However, the beginning of the Great Patriotic War and the subsequent evacuation of factories put paid to these plans. As a result, the tank troops of the Red Army entered the war without specialized engineering equipment, and with a level of mechanization lower than it had been in

1934. In effect, this would remain the case throughout the war. Nevertheless, certain steps were taken to improve the engineering equipment of tank units. On 17 July 1943 the first engineering tank regiment was formed, equipped with twenty-two T-34-76 tanks and eighteen PT-3 mine rollers. Before the end of the war seven more such regiments were formed [**56**, p. 155]. Some of the needs were met with the help of equipment received through Lend-Lease, but this was still not enough. Even in the battle for Berlin at the end of the war in Europe or the Manchurian offensive, the mechanization of sapper units was assessed as weak. Manual labour remained the main method of performance, and axes and shovels the most abundant tools.

The figures and facts given in the report on the engineering support of the 5th Shock Army in the Berlin operation speak for themselves. During the training period 41,000 small and 13,500 sapper shovels, 8,000 carpentry axes, 2,300 cross-cut saws and 390 mine detectors were issued to the troops [**57**, p. 630]. At the same time, it was noted that 'the army sappers were not sufficiently trained in working with mechanisms: diesel hammers, power tools and even the simplest means of mechanization' [**57**, p. 632]. The lack of equipment was exacerbated by the usual problems of poorly trained command staff, ill-conceived organizational structure, lack of mobility and ineffective communication.

Mobility problems were expressed in the fact that engineering reconnaissance units did not keep up with the advancing troops, resulting in delayed reports about 'obstacles, lines of enemy resistance and water obstacles' [**57**, p. 631]. In addition, corps engineers often scattered their subordinate sapper units, giving them to divisions and even regiments, but with neither means of communication, nor assistants, nor transport, they quickly lost control of them and could not, when necessary, re-assemble the sappers for use at corps level. Communication did not work effectively enough even at the level of the headquarters of the engineering troops, as the radios available in the engineering units were practically unable to work at distances over 15km [**57**, p. 632].

The need to increase the level of mechanization of engineering units was highlighted by the 5th Shock Army commanders. They saw the need 'to bolster the army's engineering brigade with machinery such as power plants, power tools, diesel hammers, sawmills, etc.' [**57**, p. 633]. In general, the need for various kinds of auxiliary equipment was frequently mentioned. Literally everything was required, from 'assault motor boats and semi-gliders capable of towing light ferries' to 'a sufficient number of smoke weapons' to provide cover from enemy aircraft [**57**, p. 634].

The problems faced by the engineer units of the 5th Shock Army were not an isolated phenomenon. The commanders of other formations noted numerous short-comings, also associated with the inadequacy of the equipment of engineering units.

So, for example, in the report on the combat actions of 2TA in the winter of 1944, the following comment is made: 'in general, the engineering units of the army, performing the tasks of engineering support, worked exclusively in difficult conditions created by muddy roads, performing the tasks manually' [**39**, p. 358].

The engineering support of the Manchurian offensive operation is of no less interest. This operation is often cited as an example of careful preparation and planning, which resulted in the defeat of the Kwantung Army. The ultimate outcome, of course, is beyond any doubt. However, it is noticeable that the technical and engineering support units suffered from the same characteristic shortcomings, known since the time of the 'Winter War': poor communications, lack of mobility and insufficient technical equipment.

'This operation clearly shows the need to [increase] the mobility of the sappers, supplying them with off-road light vehicles,' said Lieutenant Colonel Koptev, corps engineer of the 113th Rifle Corps, who took part in the Manchurian offensive [**58**, p. 275]. 'Due to the lack of transport,' he continued, 'the sapper units lagged behind and the engineering support had to be organized by involving the local population and Japanese garrisons' [**58**, p. 275]. Transport problems also influenced engineering reconnaissance. As stated in the report, 'Due to the large gap between the forward detachments and the main forces and the lack of transport for the sappers, the reports were late or did not arrive at all' [**58**, pp. 272–3]. Despite the difficult geographic conditions, the abundance of swamps, bottlenecks and the lack of roads, engineering reconnaissance played a vital role, albeit hampered by the lack of motor transport. It should be emphasized that we are not talking about the intense battles of summer 1941, but about a carefully prepared operation in August–September 1945.

The engineering support for the actions of the 6th Guards Tank Army, as the largest mechanized formation that took part in the operation, deserves separate consideration. The army had to operate in difficult conditions in terms of climate, terrain and transport infrastructure. First, up to the foothills of the Big Khingan there was a semi-desert area, then the Bain Khoshun Sume–Romin Sume–Noroharola area was very swampy with an abundance of lakes, then, in the area from Lubei to Tongliao the ground turned into a swampy semi-desert, which in the Sanchenlun area was replaced by a 10–15km wide zone of sandy hills, which proved difficult for all types of vehicles. The final 150km section from Tongliao to Zhanwu was 'extremely swampy, in places completely flooded with water' [**47**, p. 3]. In addition, the stretch of the route running along the Greater Khingan ridge had a length of 300km and was characterized as 'a great obstacle to the action of mobile forces before reaching the Central Manchzhur Plain' [**47**, p. 3].

In the army's entire zone of action some roads had limited passability in dry weather, while others were not passable for wheeled and tracked vehicles at all. In some places the abundant mountain rivers and streams became serious anti-tank obstacles in the absence of bridge-layers, because there were no bridges suitable for tanks. The underdeveloped road network and limited options for detours reduced the manoeuvrability of the tank formations and made resupply more difficult. Under such conditions, the key factors determining the success or otherwise of the tank army were uninterrupted logistic and technical support. These, in turn, directly depended on the engineering support for the operation.

The latter, according to the plans of the Soviet commanders, was divided into four groups: organization of river crossings; support in the assembly areas; support during the crossing of the Big Khingan ridge; and support on the Central Manchzhur plain. To fulfill the assigned tasks, the headquarters of the engineering troops of the 6th Guards Tank Army had various army engineering units and one front-line reinforcement brigade [**59**, p. 44].

As in the case of 2TA in the winter of 1944, the 6th Guards Tank Army followed the plan right up to the moment the offensive began. Almost immediately thereafter, the plans began to be disrupted. The engineering brigade of the front-line reinforcement unit lagged behind the advancing army and did not take any further part in the engineering support of the army's actions [**59**, p. 44]. As a result, an increased workload fell on the army engineering units, but their resources were scarce. Again several factors combined to hinder their progress, including difficult terrain, overburdening of the limited staff, insufficient resources and weak mechanization.

For example, the engineers often had to fill impassable swampy places with chippings of tuff or basalt. This was an extremely laborious process in the absence of heavy machinery. According to the report of the engineering units supporting the actions of the 6th Guards Tank Army, 'such a volume of work makes it necessary to concentrate all the army's engineering forces on overcoming the most difficult areas and to recall the engineering units supporting the forward detachments due to lack of forces. As a result, the overall pace of the army's offensive is decreasing' [**59**, p. 45].

At the end of the operation, based on the experience gained, the commanders of the engineering troops of the 6th Guards Tank Army recommended that 'the tank army, when overcoming similar, roadless and swampy terrain, should be given the most mobile front-level reinforcing units, at least a motorized engineering brigade' [**59**, p. 45].

The last stage of the route crossed the Central Manchzhur plain. The peculiarities of this area included the absence of roads and the presence of extensive wetlands and numerous rivers. During the rainy season, in late August, the rivers overflow and flood fields within a radius of 15–20km, and individual swampy areas merge into lakes, making the area almost impassable for all types of transport.

The tank army had to overcome this stretch of the route during the rainy season. Thus the commanders had no choice but to use the only railway as a road for tracked and wheeled vehicles. This method allowed them to cross the Tongliao–Zhanwu area, but it was slow (the speed of movement was only 4–5km/h) and dangerous. Besides, 'the movement on the railway track caused severe wear and tear on the materiel, excessive consumption of fuel and lubricants, as well as increased fatigue of the drivers' [**47**, p. 3 with rev.].

Finally, the mobile formation turned out to be locked in a narrow and open place. Along the sides of the route there was nothing but sands, barely passable for tracked vehicles and completely impassable for wheeled vehicles [**59**, 46]. The army was forced to advance 120km at a snail's pace, without any possibility of cover and with no chance of manoeuvring [**47**, p. 3 with rev.].

Had the enemy's air force been more active, the movement of the army would at the very least have been greatly complicated and slowed down. In the worst case scenario, the offensive would have been halted and the trapped units would have suffered serious losses. Taking into account that the 6th Guards Tank Army had been operating 700km away from the railhead at Tamtsak-Bulak [**43**, p. 40], and the weakness of the supply lines, this could have caused the failure of the entire operation.

Indeed, the stability of the army's supply chains was disrupted even without opposition from enemy forces. Documents of the 6th Guards Tank Army state that the distance of the railway from the supply depots, combined with a lack of improved roads or highways along the axis of the army's advance, constantly threatened to disrupt the supply of fuel, lubricants, ammunition and food to the combat units [**43**, p. 40]. The sum of these factors, as well as the initially insufficient equipping of the army with motor transport and repair and recovery vehicles, led to supplies being ferried in through military transport aviation. Subsequently the role of transport aviation in supplying the army was characterized as exceptional [**43**, p. 40].

Combat reports of the 6th Guards Tank Army repeatedly list the reasons for this method of supply: the long distance from the forward units to the supply base, the lack of railway lines and poor roads. Under such conditions, the reports emphasize, 'the passability of the roads became especially important' [**47**, p. 5].

Of course, the distances and the geographic and climatic conditions were known long before the operation started, and therefore the strengthening of engineering support units should have been done at the planning stage. However, as can be seen from the documentation, the army demonstrated insufficient preparedness in this regard.

All the positive changes in the equipment and organization of engineering troops date back to the early 1930s, when the active mechanization of the army began and the need for engineering support for large tank formations manifested itself. Even the relatively small successes achieved by 1934–1935 had become almost unattainable for the Red Army in the period from 1938 to 1945. In December 1934 N.I. Petin, head of the engineering department of the Red Army, said: 'The fact that the motor is introduced into the army is not the case for the engineering troops. This deprives us of the opportunity to expand the work on a wider front' [**53**, pp. 389–94].

In the period from 1938 to 1945 the level of mechanization of the engineering troops barely increased. Since 1941 the development of engineering armoured vehicles had practically stopped, and few prototypes entered mass production [**60**, pp. 408–15]. The resumption of active work on auxiliary equipment and its entry into service in massive numbers only came in the post-war period.

Conclusion

Back in 1924, M.N. Tukhachevsky's *Questions of the High Command* repeatedly highlighted the significance of command and control, communications, logistics, engineering support, reconnaissance and air defence, characterizing them as key elements of mobile warfare [**3**]. He did not focus on the technical support of the armoured forces, since at that time he considered cavalry as the mobile element of the army. However, in his later works, Tukhachevsky revised his position and switched his attention to mechanized forces. In another work, *New Questions of War*, he emphasized that the new mechanized army would require the restructuring of military logistics, and also noted that the system of repair and maintenance of equipment, along with the army's road and bridge services, would acquire great importance [**52**, pp. 191–2].

The mechanization of the army and the implementation of the Deep Operation doctrine pushed forward the need for the active development of the new system of armaments and hence the requirement for new combat and auxiliary vehicles for the mechanized formations. By the first half of the 1930s a significant number of combat and auxiliary vehicles were under development or had already entered service. Even more importantly, the Soviet military leadership had already reached a general consensus on the future of mechanized warfare. Thus, the development of the armed forces was systematic, holistic and set within the framework of a unified doctrine.

However, after Tukhachevsky and his companions were arrested and executed and the innovative doctrine was declared erroneous and 'wrecking', the development of Soviet armoured forces entered an era of constant change, which lasted uninterruptedly until 1941. With the German invasion of the Soviet Union on 22 June 1941 the situation went from bad to worse. The problems that had accumulated during the second half of the 1930s were now supplemented with new ones, which had to be fixed haphazardly with temporary and sometimes thoughtless solutions. At the same time the priorities in the development of tank forces were placed incorrectly, with some aspects being completely ignored, which resulted in an unbalanced organizational structure and excessive attention paid to the quantity of tanks and SPGs over auxiliary troops and equipment.

As can be seen from the aforementioned examples, despite persistent reports from the commanders of tank formations, Soviet tank forces in 1945 faced exactly the same problems as they had done in 1941 or even 1938. A number of deficiencies that appeared even before the Great Patriotic War haunted Soviet tank forces throughout the conflict and were not corrected until after the war or were corrected insufficiently. Some of them still exist in the modern Russian ground forces.

For example, the tank forces to some extent coped with **the problem of multiple types of tanks** in service. In the winter of 1944 the 2nd Tank Army had only three types of tanks – T-34, MK-9 (Valentine Mark IX) and KV-85 (often referred to as IS or IS-85 in the army's documents) – supplemented with three types of self-propelled guns – SU-76, SU-85 and SU-152. This was much easier to manage than the thirteen types in service in 1941 and, given the increased unification of parts and assemblies, it can be noted as a positive shift towards unification.

With proper level of **command and control**, it was possible to at least reduce, if not completely exclude, the number of unnecessary manoeuvres that wasted resources and exhausted men. However, the tank armies experienced serious difficulties in coordinating their actions not only with neighbouring formations but even among their own elements. As one can see, the situation had not radically improved in terms of command and control of the mechanized formations.

A particular problem was communications. As usual, everything went pretty well precisely until the army started the action:

> With the transfer of the army to the Stanislavchik region, organized command was immediately disrupted. By this time thawing weather had come and after tanks the roads became completely impassable. The Army's VPU [temporary command post] managed to send to the new area of operations two Willys Jeeps with two radio stations. The army headquarters stretched along the entire route and only the chief of staff of the army with a small number of operational officers moved into the new area. Wired communications and radio stations stuck along the way. During this period command and control of troops was organized mainly by radio and by sending tanks [**39**, p. 356].

The redeployment of the army to a new area followed the usual pattern: the tanks went forward, the headquarters got stuck in the mud, and communications were handled by a few radios, which they managed to drag in after the advancing troops, and by liaison officers riding on tanks.

In addition to the obvious observation that the T-34s of 2TA were used literally for every possible purpose, it is worth noting that at one point the whole tank army was protected against the collapse of the entire system of communications by a few Lend-Lease Willys Jeeps equipped with radios. As a result, the 2nd Tank Army acted as a set of loosely connected small groups of tanks, instead of as a coherent mobile formation with all its elements functioning as one.

The situation with the **repair and recovery units** remained difficult. On the one hand, more units had been formed, but on the other hand, in most cases the positive changes remained only on paper. Along with the growth in the number of repair and recovery units, the number of armoured vehicles also increased, and this, to a certain extent, countered the positive effect. At the same time, the equipment and employment of the repair and recovery units, compared to 1941, remained practically unchanged. The efficiency of the repair and recovery service, especially during manoeuvre warfare, often affected the whole course of the army's actions. For example, the commanders of 2TA emphasized that self-propelled artillery regiments should 'avoid long-distance marches as it negatively affects the accuracy and prematurely disables the weapons' [**39**, p. 364].

Likewise, the combat reports of the 8th Mechanized Corps state that lengthy forced marches without complying with basic service requirements for both vehicles and personnel were the main reasons for the loss of combat capability, and the failure of 40–50 per cent of combat vehicles for technical reasons [**61**, p. 105].

There may have been a dramatic increase in **the number of tanks and SPGs**, but neither the quality of the vehicles nor the quality of their maintenance had changed significantly compared to the pre-war period. The fact that in February 1944 the SU-85, referred to as 'the main and almost the only' effective mean of dealing with enemy heavy armour, could not be deployed over long distances for technical reasons raises a lot of questions about the standards of production and their use by the military.

The **reconnaissance units**, in terms of technical equipment, had clearly improved their capabilities, although not without foreign aid. It is worth noting that the three reconnaissance battalions of 2TA were almost completely equipped with foreign-made vehicles: British Valentine infantry tanks, American M3A half-track armoured personnel carriers and British MK-1 (Universal Carrier) multipurpose transporters [**62**, p. 144–5]. The separate reconnaissance battalion was armed with nine MK-9 tanks, six M3A armoured personnel carriers, eleven MK-1 transporters, ninety-six motorcycles, four anti-tank guns and seventeen transport vehicles [**62**, p. 144–5]. In part, this can be regarded as part of the answer to the question 'Why was Lend-Lease important?' In this particular case, without the equipment obtained under Lend-Lease, the 2nd Tank Army would not have had any combat-ready reconnaissance battalions; it would have been an army without 'eyes and ears'.

Without British and American tanks and armoured personnel carriers, reconnaissance battalions would have been equipped mainly with motorcycles, in full accordance with Khalepsky's ideas. It can be assumed that the effectiveness of such reconnaissance units would have been extremely low and hardly sufficient to meet the needs of a tank army in modern warfare.

As for the quality of the reconnaissance itself, it could be stated that the difference between the effectiveness of the reconnaissance units of the mechanized corps of 1941 and those of the tank army of 1944 is vanishingly small. As documents of

8MK note, in 1941 weak corps reconnaissance 'had a negative impact on situational awareness' [**61**, p. 105]. In 1944 documents of 2TA noted that 'haste in organizing offensive actions, excluding the minimum necessary time for reconnaissance, was the main drawback of the army's actions' [**39**, p. 361].

The next aspect requiring consideration is **air defence**. As of 16 February 1944 the tank units of 2TA had sixty-six anti-aircraft machine guns at their disposal, with no mobile air defence systems having been proposed in the late 1920s [**63**, p. 119]. The documents of 2TA highlighted that the losses from the effects of aviation in 1944 compared with 1943 were sharply reduced. During the period from 27 January to 24 February only two combat vehicles were lost from enemy aviation. The authors attributed this success to 'enhancing practical experience in camouflaging vehicles in unloading areas, during marches and in assembly areas'. However, they also conceded that the low losses were facilitated by the thaw, 'which does not allow the use of aircraft on a large scale' [**38**, p. 404]. While not denying positive changes in camouflage, it should be noted that the second factor is clearly more important than the first. If the weather had allowed the use of aircraft on a wider scale, then troops stuck on highways would become easy prey for enemy aircraft, and camouflage would not have saved them. It is worth taking into account the fact that under difficult logistic conditions, the impact of air strikes on convoys 'chained to the highways' could be fatal for the results of the whole operation.

The issue of **logistic support** for the actions of tank formations can without question be named as one of the most acute. Since there were no all-wheel-drive vehicles, tracked or half-tracked transporters in the army, 'tanks were often used to supply ammunition, fuel and lubricants' [**39**, p. 359]. Were such measures effective? For instance, the commanders of 2TA reported that 'thanks to the establishing of field supply depots, the army did not feel acute supply interruptions' [**39**, p. 359].

But what means were used to achieve this result? In the second half of February, when the enemy tried with all his might to free his encircled grouping, the army had to resort to extreme and somewhat exotic measures. 'Success depended on the manoeuvrability of the units and their support. All free transport up to staff cars was mobilized to supply front-line units with ammunition. Extreme means were brought to the issue of supporting the operation, up to using the local population, who delivered ammunition, fuel and lubricants on their shoulders' [**39**, p. 363]. It is noteworthy that the authors of the report on the hostilities of 2TA highlighted the wide use of 'all-terrain tractors' by the enemy: 'The enemy, showing particular persistence in striving to break through to the encircled grouping, resumed the offensive in the 6th Tank Army sector and, using large numbers of all-terrain tractors and tanks, succeeded somewhat and "gnawed" the way forward to the formations, reaching Chesnovka by 13.2.44' [**39**, p. 362].

Thus, the use of tanks in cooperation with auxiliary equipment was designated as one of the factors that allowed German troops to achieve a number of tactical successes. The lack of auxiliary equipment in the Soviet units, on the contrary, over-burdened their tank units and often led to their inappropriate use and the premature exhaustion of motor hours. In other words, it weakened the combat units.

Another point directly related to the effectiveness of tank formations is the presence of **motorized infantry**. Again, the example of 2TA is indicative. Each tank corps of 2TA had one motorized rifle brigade: 57MSBr with 3 Tank Corps and 15MSBr with 16 Tank Corps [**64**, p. 133]. In addition, each tank brigade included a motorized rifle battalion (in theory, a sufficient number of infantry to hold any positions captured by tanks and supporting their actions if necessary).

However, it must be understood that the motorized rifle units were moved mainly by trucks. And, like other wheeled vehicles, the trucks got stuck in the mud. Units reached the front line in dribs and drabs, often using passing tanks as 'battlefield taxis' and leaving their own artillery behind. In fact, due to the complete absence of arm-oured personnel carriers (or, at least, all-terrain vehicles), motorized rifle units were deprived of freedom of manoeuvre and, in some cases, of their firepower.

And, finally, it is worth paying attention to the most important element, which was directly or indirectly influenced by all the other factors – **people**. It's not hard to appreciate that all the aforesaid combat issues were overwhelmingly difficult for the soldiers and officers of the tank formations. They had to pay the price for all the miscalculations in organization, planning, equipment and other issues made by the higher leadership. Specifically, the absence of the necessary materiel forced people to overburden themselves. The example mentioned in the combat report of 2TA described the situation thus: 'Throughout the operation, the time needed for feeding and warming up the personnel was not taken into account, which led to the fact that, having received an order, the personnel were not physically able to carry it out' [**39**, p. 365].

The experience of the mechanized formations shows that the criticism of the ideas put forward by Tukhachevsky, Triandafillov, Kalinovsky, Egorov and other theorists in the early 1930s ultimately turned out to be untenable. The proponents of mech-anization were pretty much right.

It may seem that hasty and temporary decisions were characteristic only until the second half of 1944, and then the situation improved. However, evidence from the Manchurian operation suggests otherwise. In historical literature, the Soviet–Japanese War is often assessed as the pinnacle of the development of Soviet military thought and the result of comprehending the experience accumulated during the war with Nazi Germany. Without denying a number of really successful strategic decisions and a high, by Soviet standards, level of preparation for the operation, at the same time one cannot ignore the presence of serious shortcomings. A number of them, or at least the conditions for them, had arisen even before the start of the Second World War and some were not corrected until its very end. To a large extent, these problems were closely associated with auxiliary equipment, and the logistics and combat support of tank formations. In a number of cases it can be concluded that the Soviet high command treated these issues as secondary and did little to improve the situation, despite having opportunities to quickly resolve them. Even though the 6 Guards TA managed to maintain a high rate of advance, covering 120–140km per day, and fulfill the tasks assigned to the army, this success was largely due to the weak, patchy enemy resistance or even the complete absence of Japanese units in the tank army's offensive zone.

In general, planning of operations raises many questions. Often, if the purpose of an operation was based on controversial conclusions or unsupported assumptions, many problems could have been avoided from the outset if other decisions had been made in a timely manner. To a certain extent the operational plan of the 6th Guards Tank Army even might be considered as adventurous.

A tank army is a huge and complex organism where all elements are closely interconnected and there are simply no insignificant parts. Omissions in one place automatically cause problems in others: for example, the actions of inexperienced crews led to excessive consumption of fuel; the lack of trucks and engineering support led to interruptions (and subsequently even to a temporary failure) in supply, which in turn, necessitated the intervention of transport aviation to keep the tank army supplied. As indicated in the combat report of the 6th Guards TA, 'during the second stage of the operation, transport aviation played an important role in the delivery of fuels and lubricants' [**47**, p. 12]. The question of what would have happened to the tank army if the enemy's aircraft were active or the weather had curtailed the use of the transport aircraft remains open.

It can be seen that the shortcomings mentioned in all the aforesaid examples lie precisely within those elements mentioned by M.N. Tukhachevsky in 1924 in his work *Questions of the High Command*: namely, organizational structure, logistics, command and control, reconnaissance, etc. Thus the lack of combat and auxiliary vehicles reduced the effectiveness of the army's most powerful strike weapon.

Due to the absence of domestically produced transport and auxiliary vehicles, the key support elements of the tank formations were often armed with equipment obtained through Lend-Lease. The absence of foreign aid would have meant, at the very least, a substantial decrease in the combat capabilities of such crucial offensive forces as tank formations.

Statistics derived from the work conducted on the proving grounds of the Main Armour Directorate (GBTU) from 1931 to 1945 clearly show how the focus shifted towards tanks and self-propelled guns, omitting auxiliary and special-purpose vehicles. In total, 343 vehicles were tested during the period from 1931 to 1940; of these,

Table 16. Number of vehicles tested at the grounds of the Main Armour Directorate (GBTU) from 1931 to 1945 [**65**, p. 195].

	1931–1940		1941–1945	
Tanks and SPGs	73	21.3%	306	64.0%
Armoured Cars and APCs	26	7.6%	25	5.2%
Cars and Trucks	62	18.1%	77	16.1%
Auxiliary and Special-Purpose Vehicles	182	53.1%	70	14.6%
Total	343	100.0%	478	100.0%

182 (53.1 per cent) were auxiliary and special-purpose vehicles, and only 73 (21.3 per cent) tanks and self-propelled guns. In contrast, from 1941 to 1945 GBTU tested a total of 478 vehicles, of which 306 (64 per cent) were tanks and SPGs. Only 70 (14.6 per cent) were auxiliary and special-purpose vehicles [**65**, p. 195].

The same examples show that the shortcomings in the organization and employment of the Red Army tank forces, which manifested themselves during the pre-war conflicts and in the battles of 1941–1943, still remained at the end of 1945. Although these problems were taken into account and analysed by the high command, they were properly addressed only after the end of the war.

Photographs
1930–1940

Heavy artillery on the march during Kiev manoeuvres in September 1935. Shown are 203mm M1931 (B-4) howitzers towed by Kommunar tractors. A copy of the German Hanomag WD50 tractor, the Kommunar was designed in the early 1920s and the first example appeared in 1924. During the 1930s Kommunar tractors were used both in the military and in civil industry and were often criticized for their slow speed and mechanical unreliability. Some tractors of the type remained in military service until the end of the Great Patriotic War. *(RGVA)*

An unarmoured BKhM-1 fighting chemical vehicle (*Boyevaya Khimicheskaya Mashina*) on manoeuvres. During the 1930s Soviet engineers worked on several projects for wheeled vehicles designed for area contamination/ decontamination and laying smokescreens. These vehicles were manufactured in small numbers and saw limited use during the Winter War. *(RGVA)*

Numerous conflicts in the second half of the 1930s gave enough evidence that the Red Army needed a new type of specialized armoured vehicle to recover wounded men from the battlefield. Engineers at the DRO factory at Vyksa designed the BA-22 armoured medical transport vehicle or motorized medical aid station (*moto-medicinsky punkt*). The prototype was completed in September 1938. This photograph of a BA-22 prototype shows the armoured hull in detail. (*RGVA*)

Rear view of the BA-22 prototype showing details of the armoured hull and hinged doors. (*RGVA*)

The BA-22 moving down the 21-degree slope with the brakes on …

… and down the 27-degree slope with the brakes on. (*RGVA*)

Another view of the BA-22 armoured car during trials. It could not get out of the 200mm deep sand pit. *(RGVA)*

The prototype BA-22 was based on the GAZ-AAA (6 × 4) chassis. This model was not all-wheel-drive and that was a significant drawback for the whole project. By the beginning of the Great Patriotic War the bulk (66.9%) of the army's trucks and special-purpose vehicle fleet consisted of GAZ-AA trucks, and it had no four-wheel-drive or all-wheel-drive vehicles at all. *(RGVA)*

The BA-22 was capable of transporting twelve soldiers in summer uniform, ten lightly wounded soldiers in full equipment or four severely wounded stretcher cases. *(RGVA)*

The BA-22 had a 40hp GAZ carburettor engine. The trials confirmed that the engine was underpowered. *(RGVA)*

The BA-22 overcoming a 20-degree front slope on a dusty road. *(RGVA)*

Interestingly enough, the engineers paid much attention to the ergonomics. The BA-22 was equipped with an internal heater, as well as sufficient lighting and air vents. However, tests revealed that the ventilation system worked unsatisfactorily in the summer months. *(RGVA)*

A brand new BA-22 prototype. *(RGVA)*

In order to enhance its cross-country mobility, the prototype was equipped with optional auxiliary tracks known as 'Overall' tracks. Fitting these auxiliary tracks to the rear pair of wheels effectively converted an armoured car to a half-track. *(RGVA)*

A BA-22 prototype, showing the armoured hull in detail. Note the significant height of the vehicle (2880mm). The height was one of the reasons why the BA-22 was rejected after the trials. The report stated that the armoured vehicle was 'too tall', thus did not meet the requirements on concealment. *(RGVA)*

The BA-22 crossing a trench. Note the details of the working suspension. (*RGVA*)

A BA-22 fording a river. After the trials another drawback was noted by the commission: the hull was not dust-proof, air-proof or water proof, thus it was not suitable for chemical warfare. (*RGVA*)

(**Opposite, above**) The BA-22 prototype on a side slope. The front and side armoured flaps are opened. (*RGVA*)

(**Opposite, below**) The BA-22 prototype on a side slope. Note the sight slit with armoured flap. The hull of the vehicle had several firing ports for self-defence using personal arms. (*RGVA*)

(**Above**) Here the BA-22 is crossing a trench 1.2m wide and 0.6m deep. (*RGVA*)

(**Below**) The BA-22 about to cross the V-shaped trench. The spare wheels were also intended to act as additional support wheels in rough or uneven terrain. (*RGVA*)

The BA-22 crossing a bigger trench, 2.2m wide and 0.6m deep. Note that the rear side of the hull touches the ground. *(RGVA)*

The BA-22 prototype crossing the bigger trench. One pair of wheels has lost contact with the ground. *(RGVA)*

The same trench crossing: the silencer is touching the ground. *(RGVA)*

A drawing of the self-propelled fuel tank or STC (*Samokhodnii tank-cisterna*). Based on the T-26 chassis, it was designed at the Kirov plant (Factory No. 185) in Leningrad in 1934. The armour, suspension, power plant and transmission remained the same as on regular T-26s, and its operational range was 120km. Its main tactical role was to resupply fast-moving mechanized troops when advancing or manoeuvring. *(RGVA)*

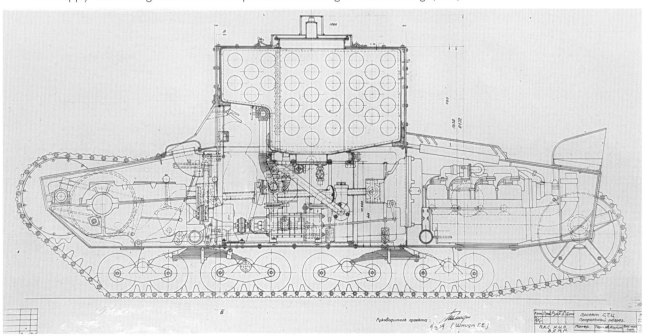

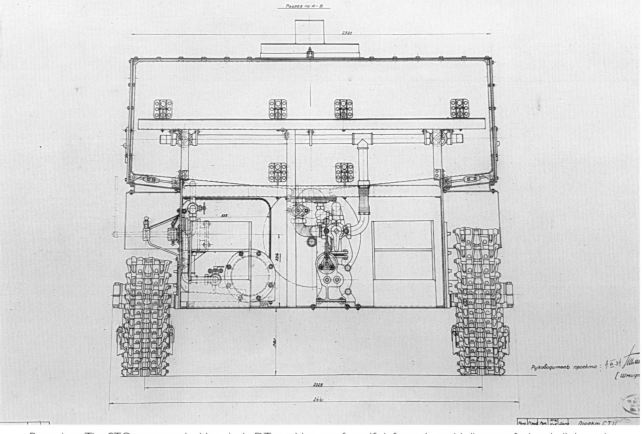

Rear view. The STC was armed with a single DT machine gun for self-defence. It could dispense fuel and oil through rubber-fabric hoses at 400 litres per minute. *(RGVA)*

A drawing of the left side of the STC. In 1936 another prototype – the TC-26 – appeared at Factory No. 174. This version had an unarmoured fuel tank with a capacity of 1,900 litres and eleven oil tanks with a capacity of 15 litres each. *(RGVA)*

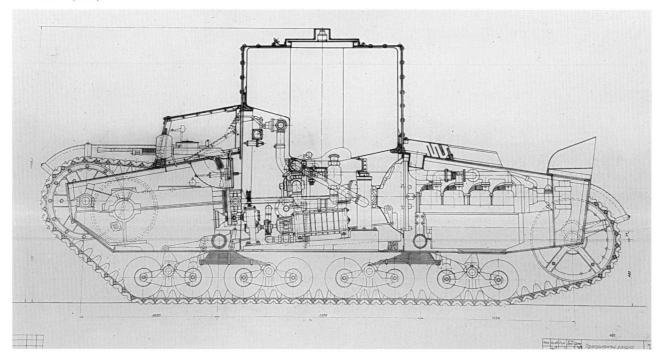

The TR-1 armoured personnel carrier was based on the T-26 and was sometimes also referred to as the TR-26 ('TR' standing for transporter). The vehicle was developed and produced in 1932/1933 at Kirov's factory in Leningrad and tested in 1934. It had a crew of one but carried up to fourteen riflemen in an armoured cabin at the back and was armed with a 7.62mm machine gun. It had 6–10mm thick armour offering all-round bullet and shell splinter protection, and a rear door for mounting and dismounting. Generally, the TR-1 had relatively high technical and tactical characteristics even by postwar standards. Trials showed that the TR1 should be adopted into service after improvements to its ergonomics and habitability. (*RGAE*)

The TPP (*Tank preodoleniya prepyatstvii*), literally 'obstacle crossing tank'. This was one of the most peculiar Russian armoured vehicles of the interwar period based on the T-26 chassis. (*RGVA*)

The TPP was designed to literally jump over obstacles by using the kinetic energy of the moving tank and eccentric gears. *(RGVA)*

The TPP was tested in 1937–1938. The results proved that the speed of the TTP, and hence its kinetic energy, was not sufficient to jump obstacles. In addiiton, the tank landed roughly, which damaged the suspension and other mechanisms. The ABTU representatives recommended that the trials be stopped and the prototype converted into a prime mover. However, they noted the TTP had some innovative engineering solutions, such as a driver's seat with a shock-absorbing mechanism and safety straps. It was recommended that this be used as standard on other Soviet tanks. *(RGVA)*

A convoy of Soviet troops with heavy artillery, pictured in Finland during the Winter War, although the exact location is unknown. In the foreground is an S-65 diesel tractor towing an artillery piece. *(RGVA)*

An OT-130 chemical tank in Finland. This photo was most probably staged. By the beginning of the Great Patriotic War the RKKA had the most numerous fleet of chemical tanks. On 22 June 1941 it had 1,059 flamethrower T-26 tanks, with 773 stationed in fourteen mobilized military districts and other 286 in Eastern military districts and on the Far Eastern Front. *(RGVA)*

Among all classes of auxiliary armoured vehicles in the RKKA, flamethrower tanks turned out to be the most tenacious class. There were versions based on the chassis of most Soviet tanks and during the Great Patriotic War they saw extensive development and were regularly improved. Pictured here is a KhT-26 during the test of the new incendiary (liquid) mixture in 1940. (TsAMO)

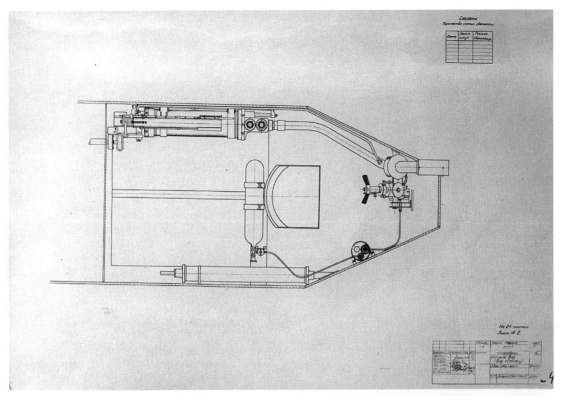

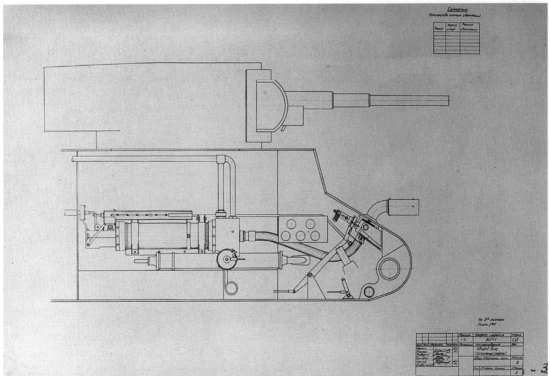

Drawings showing the installation of the flamethrower in the BT-7 tank. (*TsAMO*)

An experimental BT-7 tank with flamethrower installed. The nozzle of the flamethrower can be clearly seen under the driver's hatch. The tank was developed in late 1940/early 1941 by NATI and tested in May 1941. It was not approved for serial production because of technical drawbacks that became apparent during the trials. (*TsAMO*)

A Fougasse (*porokhovoy ognemet*) or automatic flamethrower. Flamethrowers of this type used the pressure of gases resulting from the combustion of a powder charge to throw the incendiary mixture. This type of experimental flamethrower was developed by NATI in 1941. (*TsAMO*)

A flamethrower on a stand in a test facility, 1941. (*TsAMO*)

The OU-T-26 flamethrower tank was developed in 1936 by the Military Academy of Motorization and Mechanization, and the project was supervised by famous engineer Josef Yakovlevich Kotin. It was based on a standard twin-turreted T-26 with a flamethrowing device installed on the back. (*RGVA*)

The OU-T-26 preparing to fire during trials in December 1936. *(RGVA)*

The OU-T-26 flamethrower was designed to shoot sternwards in order to protect the tank from pursuing enemy infantry. *(RGVA)*

It was able to shoot at a distance of 12–15m and held 18 litres of incendiary liquid (mixture) – enough to shoot twelve times. *(RGVA)*

The incendiary mixture burning out after the shot was made. *(RGVA)*

(**Above**) The resulting burnt-out area. (*RGVA*)

(**Opposite, above**) An SU-5-2 light self-propelled gun. It was armed with a 122mm mod.1910/30 howitzer and was based on the T-26 chassis. Development started in 1938 and by the beginning of the Great Patriotic War thirty-one had been manufactured. The SU-5-2 saw limited combat use during the conflict at Lake Khasan and in the Polish campaign in September 1939. Despite the fact that the Soviet commanders greatly appreciated their assistance at Lake Khasan, production neither sped up nor increased. (*TsAMO*)

(**Opposite, below**) An experimental SU-14 heavy self-propelled gun based on the T-35 heavy tank chassis. It was developed between 1931 and 1940 at Factory No.185. Only two prototypes were eventually manufactured. This one was armed with a 152mm M1935 (Br-2) gun. Interestingly, during the Great Patriotic War Soviet artillery did not receive any SPGs designed to provide indirect fire support. Instead, Soviet industry concentrated its efforts on producing direct fire SPGs and tank destroyers. (*TsAMO*)

In the 1930s Soviet engineers experimented with remotely controlled armoured vehicles known as teletanks (*teleupravlyaemii*). Pictured here is a group of T-20 Komsomolets remotely controlled tractors during trials in 1939. Most of the experiments were discontinued, but teletanks saw some limited combat in the Winter War. *(RGVA)*

A T-20 Komsomolets light artillery tractor. This lightly armoured vehicle was designed and tested in 1936–1937. Its primary role was to tow anti-tank artillery and regiment-level field artillery. During the Great Patriotic War it was used in various different combat roles, including as a makeshift anti-tank self-propelled gun armed with a 57mm gun, as a light machine gun tankette, and as a partisan ersatz-tank, etc. The shortage of all kinds of tractors often meant these vehicles had to tow heavier artillery systems and equipment, which led to rapid wear and frequent mechanical breakdowns. *(TsAMO)*

A Komintern medium cargo tractor and prime mover, another model designed at KhPZ in 1935. Kominterns were produced from 1934 to 1940, with 1,798 vehicles produced in all. Ironically, production of the Komintern was discontinued in 1940 due to the introduction of a new, more powerful model: the Voroshilovets. This in turn was terminated in 1941. *(TsAMO)*

An STZ cargo tractor. STZ-5 tractors were often criticized for their limited road clearance, narrow tracks, poor traction and even swinging from side to side. It had the worst off-road performance of all Soviet tracked cargo vehicles. *(TsAMO)*

(**Opposite, above**) An STZ (STZ-NATI) agricultural tractor. The STZ model went into serial production in 1937 and stayed in production until 1952. It was widely used during the war, although in essence it remained primarily an agricultural vehicle, with characteristic features such as slow speed, low off-road performance and insufficient engine power to tow tanks and heavy artillery systems. (*TsAMO*)

(**Opposite, below**) An STZ tractor at UMMC Military Museum in Verkhnyaya Pyshma. (*Author's collection*)

(**Above**) A Voroshilovets heavy tractor. This was the most powerful and advanced model of all the Soviet tractors and prime movers developed before the beginning of the Great Patriotic War. It was designed at the Kharkov Locomotive Factory (KhPZ) in 1935–1936 and after trials in 1937 was approved for serial production. Although Voroshilovets were often praised for their powerful 12-cylinder V-shaped V2-V diesel tank engines, relatively high speed (average 16km/h, maximum 42km/h) and high tractive power, they suffered from numerous defects. In 1941 production was interrupted because the factory was evacuated and subsequently never resumed. (*TsAMO*)

(**Opposite, above**) A Stalinets-2 medium artillery tractor. Designed at the ChTZ factory, the Stalinets-2 (also known as the S-2 or ST-2, from the Russian *Skorostnoy*, meaning high-speed) was first introduced in 1939 and went into serial production in September 1940. However, it turned out to be faulty and too complicated in both manufacturing and maintenance. Probably the only real advantage of the machine was its diesel engine's low fuel consumption. (*TsAMO*)

(**Opposite, below**) Another photo of the S-2 Stalinets artillery tractor. Tests revealed that the design (estimated) speed of the S-2 could only be obtained when it was moving on a highway without a load. Even minor inclines reduced its speed, while to achieve the design pulling force on the hook meant overloading the engine. (*TsAMO*)

(**Above**) An S-65 Stalinets diesel tractor. Although the S-65 turned out to be successful, it was not suitable for military service. A particular drawback was its low speed, which did not allow it to transport artillery quickly enough to keep up with fast-moving troops or tanks. (*TsAMO*)

As here, a lone Stalinets tractor would struggle to tow a T-28 medium tank on anything other than a paved road. Most often Soviet repair and recovery units used any available equipment to tow knocked-out and broken tanks, including agricultural tractors, other tanks or, more rarely, tanks converted to tractors. The latter was not officially permitted until April 1944. Consequently, the tank forces of the Red Army had no specially designed repair and recovery vehicle until 1944, except field modifications. *(RGVA)*

Komintern and Stalinets tractors towing a T-28 tank across country. The second tractor has no cabin; most likely it is a civil version. *(RGVA)*

Stalinets and Komintern tractors towing a T-28 tank uphill with a front slope of 10 per cent. Such a level of technical equipment was rarely seen in repair and recovery detachments during the Great Patriotic War. Most of the Komintern and Voroshilovets tractors were lost in the first few months of combat. *(RGVA)*

Stalinets and Komintern tractors towing a T-28 tank on a wet asphalt road. The test revealed that a single tractor could not tow a tank in such conditions as its tracks would lose traction and slide. One of the most common problems for the Soviet forces was the slow speed and underpowered engines of the recovery vehicles to hand. The average towing speed varied from 3km/h to 4–5km/h, depending on weight and road conditions. *(RGVA)*

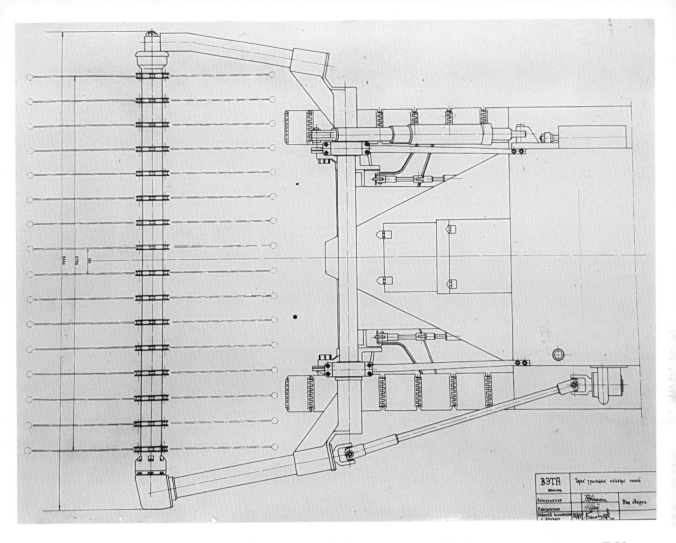

(**Opposite, above**) During tests, the Komintern and Stalinets tractors had difficulties when trying to turn a T-28 tank. A single tractor could turn the tank through 180 degrees only on a radius of 50–100m. Two tractors, however, could achieve the same manoeuvre on a radius of only 30m. *(RGVA)*

(**Opposite, below**) Two Komintern tractors towing a T-28 tank on a wet asphalt road. The most common models of tractors used by repair and recovery units were agricultural Stalinets-60s and Stalinets-65s, which were often worn-out and too underpowered to recover new models of heavy tanks and SPGs. Until the end of the Great Patriotic War Russian repair and recovery units used a mishmash of available and captured vehicles. For example, 119 Recovery and Evacuation Company should have been equipped with S-2, Komintern, Voroshilovets and Stalinets tractors. In fact, by the end of October 1944 it had in its possession only eight STZ-60/65 tractors and one STZ-3/5 tractor, and of these, only seven were serviceable. *(RGVA)*

(**Above**) The VETA mine flail, overhead view. It had become obvious in the early 1930s that tank forces needed mechanized mine-clearing equipment capable of keeping pace with mechanized troops. This mine flail for BT-5 tanks was designed in Leningrad in 1934. Its development process was lengthy, involving several design improvements. First it was developed for the BT-5, then the BT-7 and finally for the T-28. In 1939 the flail was trialled with the T-28 tank, but its performance was poor and the whole project was dropped.

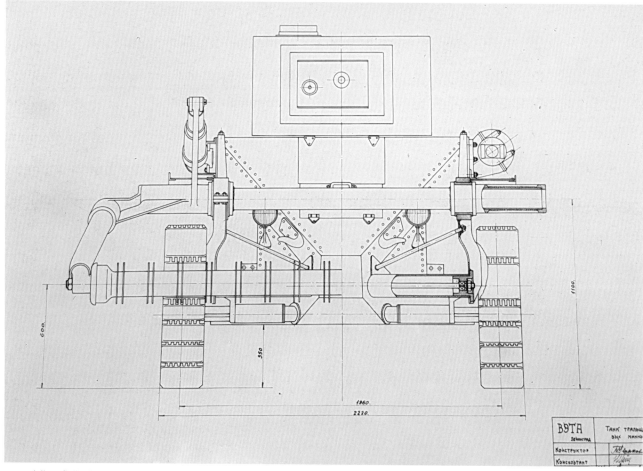

Mine flails like the VETA, along with other projects such as mine-rollers and even the futuristic 'Object 218' electrical minesweeper, were under development in the 1930 and 1940s. *(RGVA)*

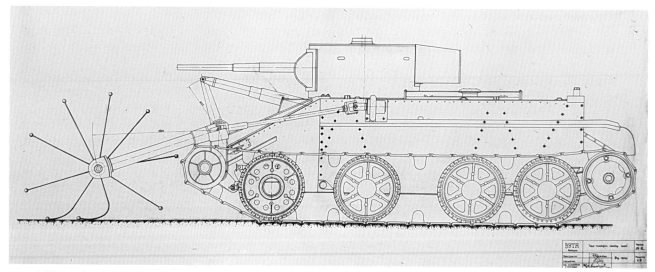

VETA mine flail, side view. *(RGVA)*

The SBT (*Sapyornii bistrokhodnii tank*), a fast-moving sapper tank, was designed in 1934–1935 by the Engineering Directorate of the RKKA. Initially it was a BT-2 tank with a bridge-laying system, designated as the SBT Model 1935. (*RGVA*)

A detached bridge. The lever mechanism was designed at the VIM factory. (*RGVA*)

(**Above**) The SBT preparing to lay the bridge. Although the project was battle-tested in Finland and generally recognized as successful, it was discontinued in 1939, probably due to the development of a new engineering tank. (*RGVA*)

An SBT about to release the bridge. The dense vegetation indicates that the vehicle was being tested in late spring or summer. The SBT had two types of bridging equipment: a 9m-long bridge without supports and two 9m long bridges with supports. *(RGVA)*

After the bridge is laid successfully, the SBT moves across the obstacle. *(RGVA)*

The SBT crossing a wide trench. Its T-38 light tank turret is clearly visible. In different versions the SBT had an armoured superstructure, a turret from the twin-turret T-26 tank, and a turret from the light amphibious T-38 tank. (*RGVA*)

A design for a bridge-laying tank based on the T-26 was initiated in 1932 by the Engineering Directorate of the RKKA. A twin-turreted T-26 tank was used as a basis for the prototype, with one turret removed to accommodate the bridge-laying equipment. (*RGVA*)

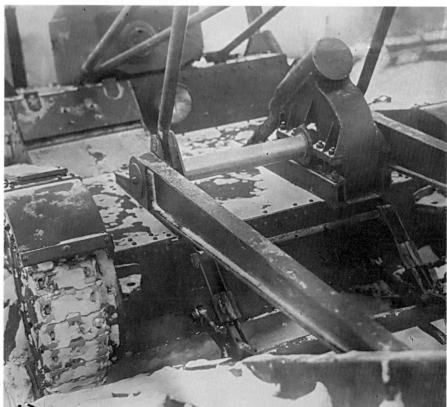

A close-up of the bridge-laying mechanism. On early prototypes one of the crew members had to be outside the vehicle when laying the bridge. It took six to seven minutes to lay the bridge. (*RGVA*)

The second prototype of the T-26-based bridge-layer was the ST-26, seen here without its bridge. After testing in 1934–1935, the tank was approved for low-rate serial production, with sixty-four vehicles manufactured. (*RGVA*)

An ST-26 preparing to lay a bridge across a river in a winter environment. The pilot series of ST-26s went to the RKKA, where tanks were tested and evaluated. A number of ST-26s saw service during the Winter War. *(RGVA)*

Moving across the stream. Testing of the ST-26 eventually led to the creation of an advanced model, the UST-26 ('U' from *usovershenstvovannii*, meaning improved or enhanced), in 1935/1936. Three prototypes were built, and further enhancement of the UST-26 continued until 1939. *(RGVA)*

This ST-26 prototype is sporting a turret from a T-38 amphibious tank. The design was eventually abandoned, although the idea of converting obsolete tanks into auxiliary vehicles was altogether good. (RGVA)

The IT-28 bridge layer was developed in 1935 at the Kirov factory in Leningrad. Two prototypes were produced (in 1935 and 1940) and handed over for trials. The design was based on a turretless T-28 medium tank. (RGVA)

At the end of 1940 the IT-28 was adopted into service and approved for low-rate initial production, with the first batch to consist of fifty-five tanks. Due to the outbreak of the war and the evacuation of the Kirov factory, this plan was never completed. *(RGVA)*

An IT-28 model 1940, the second prototype, pictured at the NIBT proving grounds in 1940, without a bridge . . . *(RGVA)*

... and with a bridge. *(RGVA)*

The IT-28 model 1940 was armed with two 7.62mm machine guns. The mounts are clearly visible to the left and right of the driver's position. *(RGVA)*

The IT-28 prototype crossing the 6.5m wide trench. One bridge span allowed the tank to cross obstacles up to 12m wide, and 4.5m escarpments. *(RGVA)*

Laying the bridge over the 6.5m wide trench. Using several sequentially connected 12m bridge spans allowed obstacles up to 48m wide to be crossed. *(RGVA)*

The IT-28 during trials in 1940, moving towards a 7m high obstacle. The bridge is raised and ready to be placed in position. *(RGVA)*

An IT-28 tank crawling up its own bridge. Note that the wooden surface of the bridge has been partially destroyed by the tracks. *(RGVA)*

The IT-28 with the bridge, rear view. Another important feature of the design was the ability to mount cargo cranes on the tank, which could be used to recover light tanks from up to 10m deep trenches, as well as to recover stuck vehicles – armoured and unarmoured – from rivers and swamps, etc. *(RGVA)*

The IT-28 model 1940 with the bridge elevated. Another feature of the IT-28 was the ability to attach a mine trawl to clear passages through enemy minefields and barbed-wire entanglements. Its range of capabilities made the IT-28 a fully fledged engineering tank. *(RGVA)*

Photographs
1941–1945

The T-50 prototype, armed with a flamethrower. The project for a new infantry support tank was initiated in 1939 by the OKMO design bureau at the S.M. Kirov Factory No. 185. After the OKMO was decimated during the Great Purge, the project was transferred to the K.E. Voroshilov Factory No. 174 in Leningrad. The flamethrower version was designed and subsequently tested there in March–April 1941. *(TsAMO)*

The flamethrower mounted on the T-50. *(TsAMO)*

A more detailed image of the flamethrower mounted on the T-50. (*TsAMO*)

The first in a sequence of five photographs of a T-50 tank demonstrating the use of the flamethrower on the move. It produced a wall of flame, and the incendiary mixture burned spectacularly. (*TsAMO*)

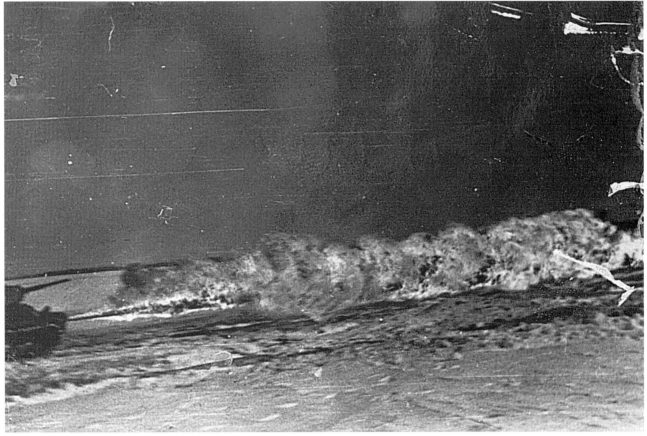

A T-50 tank demonstrating the use of the flamethrower from a stationary position. (*TsAMO*)

The residue of the incendiary mixture burning out on the flamethrower's nozzle. (*TsAMO*)

The flamethrower mount near the ammunition stowage. (*TsAMO*)

The armoured mantlet on the OT-34 with OP-34 flamethrower. Left to right: mantlet, armoured ball mount, and the flamethrower's nozzle. (*TsAMO*)

Колпак бронировки   Шар бронировки   Сопло с фланцем

A T-34 tank equipped with the OP-34 flamethrower. The flamethrower mount replaced the standard DT machine gun. (*TsAMO*)

The OP-34 flamethrower position inside a T-34-76 tank. (*TsAMO*)

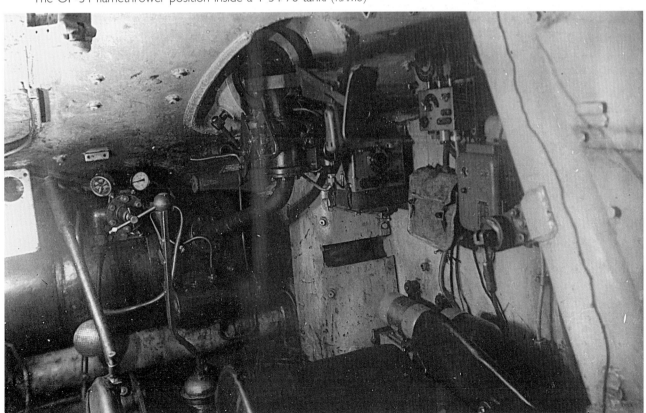

Trials of the OP-34 flamethrower. A T-34-76 tank demonstrates the use of the flamethrower in a stationary position (top) and on the move (bottom), 7 April 1943. (*TsAMO*)

A T-34 preparing to fire an OP-34 flamethrower, 7 April 1943. A flame torch is visible. (*TsAMO*)

The OT-34-85 (*Ognemyotnii tank*, flame-throwing tank) was developed in 1944 at Factory No. 174 in Omsk. It was adopted into service and entered serial production in July 1944. By the end of the Great Patriotic War a total of 331 OT-34-85s had been produced. (*TsAMO*)

The T-60-based SPAAG prototype, left side. The first combat engagements of the war had painfully exposed the fact that Soviet tank forces were in desperate need of mobile means of air defence in the form of self-propelled anti-aircraft guns. Development of the T-60 SPAAG (also referred to as the T-60 *zenitnii*, or anti-aircraft) started in 1942 at the GAZ Factory in Gorky (now Nizhny Novgorod) and at Factory No. 37 in Sverdlovsk (now Yekaterinburg). It was one of several attempts to develop an armoured vehicle with a dedicated anti-aircraft capability. (*RGAE*)

The SPAAG prototype was based on the basic model of a T-60 light tank but with a new open-topped turret. It was armed with two 12.7mm DShK machine guns on a twin mount. The disadvantages of the prototype were obvious: the turret was too cramped and its layout was awkward, with poor gun laying and turret traverse speed. Due to the numerous defects the project was dropped. *(RGAE)*

The prototype of the T-70 SPAAG. This was another unsuccessful attempt to enhance the anti-aircraft capability of the Soviet tank forces. *(RGAE)*

The T-70 SPAAG was also armed with two 12.7mm DShKT machine guns on a twin mount. In December 1942 the prototype was tested, but with unsatisfactory results. Numerous design flaws were noted, specifically the cramped turret, difficult targeting and an unstable gun mount which caused poor accuracy. Eventually, the project was cancelled. *(RGAE)*

Men of the 1st Artillery Division of the Reserve of the Supreme High Command (RGK) pictured loading a GAZ-AA *polutorka* truck onto a train before moving from Stalingrad to the Central Front in 1943. Despite all efforts to develop and adopt improved models, the GAZ-AA and ZIS-5 remained the most numerous models of trucks during the Second World War. *(TsAMO)*

Units of the 1st Artillery Division of the RGK moving to new positions in the summer of 1943. Here, a Stalinets-65 (also referred as S-65 or ChTZ-65) tractor is towing an artillery piece. According to the 1940 plan, the S-60 and S-65 agricultural tractors were to be replaced with more advanced models, the ST-2 and T-34-based armoured tractor. However, this plan was never implemented and obsolete models remained in service until the end of the war. (*TsAMO*)

An STZ-5 artillery tractor towing a 122mm howitzer and a limber, with the gun crew riding on the back of the tractor and on the limber. This photograph was taken as units of the 2nd Guards Artillery Brigade moved from the Dmitrov-Orlovsky sector to the Sevsk sector. (*TsAMO*)

The same unit, but the date of the photograph is unknown. Here, an STZ-5 artillery tractor is towing a 122mm howitzer and a trailer. STZ-5 tractors were widely used in the RKKA, but they were slow and underpowered and not suitable for towing artillery in extreme conditions. *(TsAMO)*

The STZ-5, also designated the STZ-5 Stalinets or STZ-5-NATI, was produced at the Stalingrad Tractor Plant between 1937 and 1942. Based on its agricultural model, it was often criticized for its slow speed (10–14km/h), poor cross-country ability and low power to weight ratio. Nonetheless, the STZ-5 was one of the most produced prime movers, with 9,944 manufactured before and during the Great Patriotic War. *(TsAMO)*

Units of the 1st Artillery Division of the RGK on their way to new positions. Shown here are two camouflaged STZ-5 prime movers towing guns. (TsAMO)

A Ya-12 fast-moving tractor towing a 122mm D2 gun. The Ya-12 was designed at the Yaroslavl Motor Plant and was manufactured from 1943 to 1946, with a total production of 2,296 tractors, 2,249 of them produced before the end of the war. The production of its predecessor, the Ya-11, had had to be stopped owing to a lack of engines. In turn, the Ya-12 used a US-built engine, the GMC-4-71, a Long-32 clutch and Spicer-5553 gearbox. (TsAMO)

A Ya-12 tractor tugs a 122mm D2 gun through a wide trench in winter. (*TsAMO*)

Another attempt to enhance the mobility of artillery units, the BM-8-16 'Katyusha' Multiple Launch Rocket System (MLRS) on an STZ5-NATI tractor chassis at the UMMC Military Museum in Verkhnyaya Pyshma. (*Author's collection*)

(**Above**) It was a far from ideal solution as the tractor retained all its shortcomings, including poor off-road mobility and swinging. Thus, the MLRS had poor accuracy and in fact was more of a psychological weapon. (*Author's collection*)

(**Opposite, above**) The PT-3 (*protivominnii tral*, anti-mine trawl) mine roller was developed in 1941/1942 by Engineer Pavel Mugalev. The first models were adopted in 1943, and in 1944 the PT-3 was enhanced and in the course of 1944–1945 the roller saw trials with various models of tanks, including the T-34-85, T-44, IS-2 and IS-3. Pictured here is a T-34-85 equipped with a PT-3 mine roller during trials at the Kubinka proving grounds in 1945. In comparison to the US mine trawls T1-E3 and T1-E4, the PT-3 trawl was significantly lighter (only 5.3 tons) and could be attached without using any auxiliary equipment. The second advantage of the PT-3 model was that a tank could still use its armament when trawling, although not without constraints. (*TsAMO*)

(**Opposite, below**) A T-44 equipped with a PT-3 mine roller during trials at the Kubinka proving grounds in 1945. Despite the fact that the PT-3 had been in service since 1943, these trials revealed some production and design defects. Specifically, the trawl made it impossible to use the tank's main armament when firing forward, and restricted visibility for the driver. (*TsAMO*)

An experimental M-4 quad mortar mount on a ZIS-5 chassis. The desire to enhance the mobility and firepower of the artillery often led to strange designs. This quad mortar had a crew of nine. The truck was intended only to transport the crew and mortar, and was not armoured. (*TsAMO*)

A Studebaker US6 truck towing a 122mm D2 gun. Studebakers (often called 'Studer' by Russian soldiers) were the most numerous type of truck supplied to the Soviet Union under the Lend-Lease agreement. (*TsAMO*)

An IS-3 heavy tank with tank riders, or *tank desant*, on it. According to official documents the IS-3 tank could accommodate up to twelve infantrymen. *(TsAMO)*

The same IS-3 heavy tank seen from the rear. The tank riders sat very close to each other, grouped behind the turret. Some of them look utterly unprotected. *(TsAMO)*

This post-war photograph shows a T-34-85 with eleven infantrymen onboard. The *tankovy desant* assault tactic was commonly known and widely used by the Red Army during the Great Patriotic War and for some time after the war. In some cases the tactic proved very useful, but it remained extremely dangerous and inflexible, since after dismounting the infantry had to rely on their own strength and luck. If the tank attack was repelled, they were left without protection and means to retreat or to recover wounded comrades. (*TsAMO*)

A T-34-85 with 11 infantrymen onboard, seen from the front. (*TsAMO*)

Soviet *tank desant* on an ISU-152. Early models of the Soviet SPGs were not equipped with machine guns or any other self-defence armament. Thus, clumsy and slow SPGs were completely defenceless in close combat. Consequently, it became common practice to attach three to five infantrymen to every SPG for protection against enemy troops, as well as helping crews with everyday duties and maintenance. (*TsAMO*)

Twelve Soviet soldiers enjoying themselves on the back of an ISU-152 self-propelled gun. (*TsAMO*)

An SU-76M SPG with seven soldiers on it. Riding on tanks and SPGs was dangerous even in non-combat conditions. Weather conditions, dust, exhaust fumes, dense vegetation and low branches all created a hazard to riders. *(TsAMO)*

Perhaps the same SU-76M with tank riders, seen from the front. As infantry support was not always available, SPG crews willingly used captured enemy machine guns for close protection against enemy infantry. *(TsAMO)*

An SU-100 with tank riders, seen from the front. (*TsAMO*)

An SU-100 with five tank riders, seen from the back. (*TsAMO*)

(**Opposite, above**) A convoy of two Soviet SU-76Ms and a Willys jeep on the march somewhere in the Vyborg region on the Karelian Isthmus. No date is given, but it was probably in the summer of 1944. The image shows tank riders in vivid detail. It was a very common and yet extremely dangerous tactic, as well as a method of transporting troops. (*NARA*)

(**Opposite, below**) The absence of domestically produced armoured personnel carriers in the RKKA and the urgent need to increase protection for the tank riders during assaults resulted in a number of makeshift and even bizarre designs. Pictured here is a T-34-76 tank equipped with two open-topped armoured gondolas for infantrymen on the left and right fenders and a troop compartment at the back. Both gondolas have firing ports. (*TsAMO*)

(**Above**) An armoured open-topped superstructure was mounted at the back. A hinged door for mounting and dismounting and at least four firing ports are visible, all facing to the back. Obviously the ports were intended to provide suppressive fire when the tank was stationary. The efficiency of the whole design seems highly dubious, as the compartment at the back would not have protected the troops within against shrapnel and splinters. During an assault the troops were supposed to lay down very close to the exhaust pipes. (*TsAMO*)

Ремонтный танк ч/б М·3 средний

(**Above**) The T2 Tank Recovery Vehicle was a relatively rare modification of the M3 medium tank. A limited number of T2 ARVs was supplied to Soviet Union and tested there, but the Soviets were not satisfied either with the M3 medium tank nor with the T2 ARV, and characterized them as 'low quality' armoured vehicles unsuitable for service and wide use. However, the USSR still did not have its own domestically produced ARVs by the end of the war. Some Soviet reports stressed that 'the equipment of the Soviet army falls behind all foreign armies in terms of all types of auxiliary equipment'. (*TsAMO*)

(**Opposite, above**) A Valentine III bridge-layer at the Kubinka proving grounds. Only twenty-five were supplied to the USSR, but it performed exceptionally well and was highly appreciated by Soviet tankers. The Valentine bridge-layer carried a 30ft scissor bridge that could carry relatively heavy loads: over 30 tons (class 30). Further tests revealed it would be possible to use the vehicle with most of the Soviet heavy tanks, including the IS-family. (*TsAMO*)

(**Opposite, below**) The M19 tank transporter system consisted of an M20 Diamond T Model 980 truck with an M9 trailer. The Soviet Union received a certain quantity of heavy trucks and trailers, and tested them at the Kubinka proving grounds. US heavy trucks saw service with the RKKA and, according to Soviet reports, performed superbly as a means of transporting heavy armoured vehicles and as recovery vehicles. Reports from Kubinka also stressed the fact that no factories in the USSR were involved in the production or development of heavy trucks and trailers, despite the Red Army's great need of such vehicles. (*TsAMO*)

Sources

1. Vremennyi Polevoi Ustav RKKA, PU-36 [Temporary Field Regulations, 1936]. Gosudarstvennoye voyennoye izdatelstvo Narkomata Oborony SSSR, Moskva, 1937.

2. Habeck, Mary R. *Storm of Steel: The Development of Armor Doctrine in Germany and the Soviet Union, 1919–1939.* Cornell University Press, 2003.

3. Tukhachevskii M.N. 'Voprosy vysshego komandovaniya', Izbrannye proizvedeniya. V 2-h t. ['Questions of Higher Command', Selected Works, 2 vols, pp. 187–9]. M.: Voenizdat, 1964, ss. 187–9.

4. Raport Malinovskogo, 'Operativno-takticheskie vyvody i zakljucheniya, sdelannye na osnovanii boevogo opyta vojny v Ispanii za period ot nachala mjatezha po maj 1938 goda' [Malinovsky's report, 'Operative-tactical conclusions drawn from the war in Spain from the beginning of the rebellion to the end of May 1938']. RGVA, F. 35082, Op. 1, D. 483, L. 35.

5. Raport Mereckova i Simonova Voroshilovu i Shaposhnikovu, 5 avgusta 1937 goda [A report from Mereckov and Simonov to Voroshilov and Shaposhnikov, 5 August 1937]. RGVA, F. 33987, Op. 3, D. 1015, LL. 234–49.

6. Ryzhakov, A. 'K voprosu o stroitel'stve bronetankovyh vojsk Krasnoj Armii v 30-e gody' ['On the question of building the armoured forces of the Red Army in the 1930s']. VIZh, #8 (Avgust 1968).

7. Stenogramma vechernego zasedanija 10 Dekabrja 1934 g. [Transcript of the evening meeting on 10 December 1934]. RGVA. F. 4, Op. 18, D. 51, LL. 103–4. Citiruetsja po. Istochnik: Voennyj sovet pri NKO SSSR. Dekabr' 1934 g.: Dokumenty i materialy [Cited after: Military Council with the People's Commissariat for Defence of the USSR, December 1934: Documents and resources]. – M.: 'ROSSPEN', 2007, ss. 129–92.

8. Raport Khalepskogo Voroshilovu, 'Ob organizacii Avto-Bronetankovyh vojsk RKKA', 14 Janvarja 1935 goda [A report from Khalepsky to Voroshilov, 'On the organization of the Armoured Forces of RKKA', 14 January 1935]. RGVA, F. 4, Op. 14, D. 1411, LL. 21–3, 26–7.

9. Raport Khalepskogo Voroshilovu, 'Ob organizacii Avto-Bronetankovyh vojsk RKKA', 14 Janvarja 1935 goda [A report from Khalepsky to Voroshilov, 'On the organization of the Armoured Forces of RKKA', 14 January 1935]. RGVA, F. 4, Op. 14, D. 1411, LL. 17–18.

10. Raport Khalepskogo Voroshilovu, 'Ob organizacii Avto-Bronetankovyh vojsk RKKA', 14 Janvarja 1935 goda [A report from Khalepsky to Voroshilov, 'On the organization of the Armoured Forces of RKKA', 14 January 1935]. RGVA, F. 4, Op. 14, D. 1411, LL. 18–20.

11. Zapiska Egorova komandujushim okrugov, 2 fevralja 1935 [A memo from Egorov to district commanders, 2 February 1935]. RGVA, F. 31811, Op. 2, D. 461, LL. 153–4.

12. Protokol #29, 'O sisteme tanko-traktoro-avtobrone-vooruzhenija RKKA, 1 avgusta 1929 goda' [Minute #29, 'On the system of tank-tractor-auto-armoured weapons of RKKA', 1 August 1929]. RGVA, F. 31811, Op. 1, D. 7, LL. 1–2 s ob.

13. O sisteme tanko-traktoro-avto-brone-vooruzhenija RKKA, 5 ijunja 1929 goda [On the system of tank-tractor-auto-armoured weapons of RKKA, 5 June 1929]. RGVA, F. 4, Op. 2, D. 504, LL. 5–18 s ob.

14. Tuhachevskij Stalinu, dekabr' 1930 [From Tukhachevsky to Stalin, December 1930]. RGVA, F. 33987, Op. 3, D. 400, LL. 74–9.

15. Otchet po zagranichnoj komandirovke nachal'nika UMM RKKA i Predsedatelja Komissii – I. Halepskogo, 6 ijunja 1930 g [Report on the trip abroad of the head of the UMM RKKA and the Chairman of the Commission – I. Khalepsky, 6 June 1930]. RGVA, F. 31811, O.1, D.7, LL. 35–49.

16. Zapiska Halepskogo Tuhachevskomu, 'Takticheskie trebovanija, opredeljajushhie sistemu tankovogo vooruzhenija RKKA', vesna 1931 goda [Memo from Khalepsky to Tukhachevsky, 'Tactical requirements defining the system of tank armaments of the Red Army', Spring 1931]. RGVA, F. 31811, Op. 2, D. 77, LL. 14–15.

17. Zapiska Tuhachevskogo Halepskomu, 3 marta 1931 goda [Memo from Tukhachevsky to Khalepsky, 3 March 1931]. RGVA, F. 31811, Op. 1, D. 101, LL. 18–22.

18. Spravka komissii prezidiuma TsK KPSS, 'O proverke obvinenij, pred'javlennyh v 1937 godu sudebnymi i partijnymi organami tt. Tuhachevskomu, Jakiru, Uborevichu i drugim voennym dejateljam, v izmene rodiny, terrore i voennom zagovore', Ne pozdnee 26 ijulja 1964 g. [Note of the Commission of the Presidium of the Central Committee of the CPSU, 'On the verification of the charges brought in 1937 by the judicial and party bodies against Tukhachevsky, Yakir, Uborevich and other military leaders, for treason, terror and military conspiracy', 26 July 1964]. Opublikovano: Voennye arhivy Rossii. 1993. Vyp. 1, s. 4–113; Voenno-istoricheskij arhiv, 1998. Vyp. 2, s. 3–81.

19. Stenogramma zasedanija Voennogo soveta pri narkome oborony SSSR (Vechernee zasedanie 21 nojabrja 1937 g) [Transcript of the meeting of the Military Council under the USSR People's Commissar of Defence (Evening meeting on 21 November 1937)]. RGVA, F. 4, Op. 18, D. 54, LL. 45–61.

20. Raport Pavlova, 'Otchet ob itogah boevoj podgotovki avto-bronetankovyh vojsk RKKA za 1938 god', 20 nojabrja 1938 goda [Pavlov's report, 'Report on the results of combat training of the auto-armoured forces of the Red Army for 1938', 20 November 1938]. RGVA, F. 31811, O. 2, D. 849, L. 31.

21. 17 ijulja 1937 g. – Dokladnaja zapiska voennoj gruppy Komissii partijnogo kontrolja sekretarju CK VKP(b) I.V. Stalinu o polozhenii v tankovoj promyshlennosti [17 July 1937 – Memorandum of the military group of the Party Control Commission to the Secretary of the Central Committee of the All-Union Communist Party of Bolsheviks I.V. Stalin on the situation in the tank industry]. AP RF, F. 3, Op. 46, D. 383, LL. 121–5. Podlinnik, citiruetsja po: Stanovlenie oboronno-promyshlennogo kompleksa SSSR (1933–1937). M. 2011, str. 678–80.

22. 'Novoe lico Krasnoj armii' – stat'ja iz nemeckogo zhurnala 'Wehrfront' (# 24). Ijun' 1937 g. ['The new face of the Red Army', article from the German magazine *Wehrfront* (No. 24, June 1937)]. RGVA, F. 33987, Op. 3, D. 1080, LL. 7–11. Mashinopisnyj jekz. perevoda na russkij jazyk. Otp[echatano] 2 ekz [A typewritten copy of the translation to Russian].

23. Gosudarstvennyj komitet oborony SSSR (GKO), Dokument 2791ss. O sformirovanii 10 tankovyh armij, 28.01.1943 [USSR State Defence Committee (GKO), Document 2791ss. On the formation of 10 tank armies, 28 January 1943]. RGASPI, F. 644, Op. 1, D. 84, LL. 63–84.

24. Polevoj Ustav RKKA (PU-39) [RKKA Field Regulations, 1939]. Gosudarstvennoe Voennoe Izdatel'stvo Narkomata Oborony Sojuza SSR. Moskva, 1939 god.

25. Spravka Avtobronetankovogo upravlenija RKKA o sisteme avtobronetankovogo vooruzhenija v tret'ej pjatiletke – 15 dekabrja 1938 g [Note of the Red Army Armoured Directorate on the system of armoured vehicles in the third five-year plan, 15 December 1938]. RGVA, F. 31811, Op. 3, D. 400, LL. 79–81, ob. Zaverennaja kopija.

26. Sistema vooruzhenij 1940 – Postanovlenija Glavnogo voennogo soveta RKKA o sistemah vooruzhenija RKKA [The system of armaments 1940 – Resolutions of the Main Military Council of the Red Army on systems of armaments of the Red Army]. RGVA, F. 4, O. 14, D. 2631, LL. 138–45.

27. Perepiska s General'nym shtabom RKKA, Komitetom Oborony SNK SSSR i Centralnimi upravlenijami RKKA o planah nauchno-issledovatel'skih oboronnyh rabot narkomatov na 1940 g [Correspondence with the General Staff of the Red Army, the Defence Committee of the Council of People's Commissars of the USSR and the Central Directorates of the Red Army about the plans for research and development works on defence projects of the People's Commissariats for 1940]. RGVA, F. 4, O. 14, D. 2800, L 28.

28. Avtomobil'nyj park Krasnoj armii, 28 sentjabrja 1945 goda [Automotive fleet of RKKA, 28 September 1945]. TsAMO, F. 41, Op. 11584, D. 395, LL. 10–90.

29. Sostojanie tankovogo vooruzhenija i neobhodimost' sozdanija novyh klassov tankov, 28 janvarja 1941 g [The state of tank armaments and the need to create new classes of tanks, 28 January 1941]. TsAMO, F. 38, O. 11355, D. 224, LL. 1–59.

30. Dokument 5568s. Rasporjazhenie. Ob organizacii proizvodstva tjagachej na baze tanka T-34 na tankoremontnyh zavodah Narkomata oborony [Document 5568s. Order. On the organization of production of tractors based on the T-34 tank at the tank repair plants of the People's Commissariat of Defence]. RGASPI, F. 644, Op. 2, D. 304, L. 178.

31. Interview of Kryat Viktor Mikhaylovich by A. Drabkin, edited by N. Anichkin (31 August 2012). Retrieved from: https://iremember.ru/memoirs/tankisti/kryat-viktor-mikhaylovich/.

32. Soljankin, A.G., Pavlov, M.V., Pavlov, I.V., Zheltov, I.T. Tom 1. Otechestvennye bronirovannye mashiny. 1905–1941 gg. [*Domestic Armoured Vehicles*, vol. 1, *1905–1941*]. M.: OOO Izdatel'skij centr 'Eksprint', 2002, 344 s.: il.

33. 1-ja nauchnaja konferencija Akademii sovmestno s vrachami Privolzhskogo voennogo okruga 28-30 maja 1940 g. [Tekst]: Sanitarnoe obespechenie boevyh dejstvij roty i batal'ona: Plan i tezisy dokladov (First scientific conference of the Academy together with the doctors of the Privolzhskii Military District on 28–30 May 1940 [Text]: Sanitary support of the company and battalion combat operations: Plan and theses of reports]. Kujb. voenno-med. akad. Kr. Armii. - Kujbyshev: [b. i.]. 1940, 40 s.

34. 'Spravka o sostojanii tankovogo parka ABT-vojsk Jugo-Zapadnogo Fronta', dokument: 1/00287, 31.01.1942 g ['Information about the state of the tank fleet of the ABT troops of the South-Western Front', document 1/00287, 31 January 1942]. TsAMO, F. 229, O. 161, D. 819, LL. 32–7.

35. Karpenko, A. 'Sovershenstvovanie tehnicheskogo obespechenija bronetankovyh vojsk v operacijah' ['Improving the technical support of armoured forces in operations']. Voenno-istoricheskij zhurnal, #4, 1967, ss. 15–23.

36. Evakuacija i remont tankov 3 TA v period zimnih operacij. Janvar' – Aprel' 1943 g [Evacuation and repair of 3rd TA tanks during winter operations. January–April 1943]. TsAMO, F. 316, O. 4487, D. 98, LL. 1–9.

37. Itogi nastupatelnyh i oboronitelnyh deystvii 3 TA na uchastke VorF [The results of offensive and defensive actions of the 3rd TA in the Voronezh Front sector]. TsAMO, F. 203, O. 2843, D. 487/1, LL. 101–3.

38. Otchet upravlenija bronetankovogo snabzhenija i remonta o boevyh dejstvijah 2 TA, 10.10.1944 g [Report of the department of supply and repair of the armoured forces on the combat actions of 2 TA]. TsAMO, F. 307, O. 4148, D. 224, LL. 401–8.

39. Doklad o boevyh dejstvijah 2 TA v sostave 1 Ukrainskogo fronta s 25.01.1944 po 25.02.1944 g., 15.10.1944 g [Report on the combat operations of the 2nd TA within the 1st Ukrainian Front from 25 January 1944 to 25 February 1944]. TsAMO, F. 307, O. 4148, D. 224, LL. 329–400.

40. As in the document. Further and in other documents, the correct toponym is used – Sinarny or Sinarna, a village in the Oratovsky district of the Vinnytsia region. See example in: Zhurnal boevyh dejstvij 2 TA, 11.10.1944 g [War Diary of the 2nd Tank Army, 11 October 1944]. TsAMO, F. 307, O. 4148, D. 1, L. 90.

41. Ukomplektovannost' avtotransportom 2 TA, 01.02.1944 g. [Availability of the automotive vehicles in 2nd TA, 1 February 1944]. TsAMO, F. 307, O. 4148, D. 263, L. 7.

42. Spravka o nalichii i teh. sostojanii samohodnoj artillerii 2 TA [Note on the availability and technical condition of self-propelled artillery in 2nd TA]. TsAMO, F. 307, O. 4148, D. 245, L. 76.

43. Nastupatel'naja operacija 6 gv. TA ZabF, 31.08.1945 g [Offensive operation of the 6 Guards Tank Army of the Zabaikalsky Front, 31 August 1945]. TsAMO, F. 339, O. 5179, D. 130, LL. 1–43.

44. Kampanija Sovetskih Vooruzhennyh sil na Dal'nem Vostoke v 1945 godu. Fakty i cifry [Campaign of the Soviet armed forces in the Far East in 1945. Facts and Figures]. Voenno-istoricheskij zhurnal, #8, 1965, ss. 64–73.

45. Otchet o tehnicheskom obespechenii boevyh operacij 6 gv. TA s 08.08.1945 po 31.08.1945 g [Report on the technical support of combat operations of the 6th Guards. TA from 8 August 1945 to 31 August 1945]. TsAMO, F. 339, O. 5179, D. 98, LL. 47–54.

46. Doklad-otchet o provedennom marshe 5 gv. tk s 11 po 14.7.45 goda, 05.08.1945 g. [Report on the 5th Guards Tank Corps march from 11 July to 14 July 1945]. TsAMO, F. 339, O. 5179, D. 69, L. 191–200.

47. Doklad o boevyh dejstvijah 6 gv. TA s 09.08.1945 po 23.08.1945 g., 23.08.1945 g [Combat Report on the actions of the 6th Guards TA from 9 August 1945 to 23 August 1945]. TsAMO, F. 339, O. 5179, D. 98, LL. 1–43.

48. Vedomost' o nalichii i tehsostojanii avtomashin 7 MK, 30.09.1945 g [Statement of the availability and technical condition of automotive transport of 7 MK, 30 September 1945]. TsAMO, F. 339, O. 5179, D. 132, L. 171.

49. Loza, D.F. 'Tankist na "inomarke"' [Memoirs of Hero of the Soviet Union Dmitriy Loza]. Eksmo, 2007 g., s. 320.

50. Doklad o dejstvijah aviacii protivnika i chastej PVO 6 gv. TA ZabF za avgust mesjac 1945 goda, 31.08.1945 g [Report on the actions of enemy aviation and air defence units of the 6th Guards TA ZabF for the month of August 1945, 31 August 1945]. TsAMO, F. 339, O. 5179, D. 93, LL. 191–200.

51. Nazarenko, K.B. 'Mihail Nikolaevich Tuhachevskij: mezhdu mifami i istoricheskoj naukoj' ['Mikhail Nikolaevich Tukhachevsky: between myths and historical science']. Novejshaja istorija Rossii, #3, 2015, s. 62.

52. Tuhachevskij, M.N. 'Novye voprosy vojny'. Izbrannye proizvedenija. V 2-h t. [Tukhachevsky, M.N. 'New Questions of War'. Selected Works. In two volumes]. M.: Voenizdat, 1964, ss. 180–92.

53. Stenogramma utrennego zasedanija 12 dekabrja 1934 g., 1934.12.12 [Transcript of the morning meeting on 12 December 1934]. RGVA, F. 4, Op. 18, D. 51, LL. 389–94. Citiruetsja po: Voennyj sovet pri NKO SSSR. Dekabr' 1934 g.: Dokumenty i materialy [Cited after: Military Council with the People's Commissariat for Defence of the USSR, December 1934: Documents and resources]. M.: 'ROSSPEN', 2007, ss. 313–97.

54. Birjukov, P.I. i dr. Inzhenernye vojska. Uchebnik. [Engineering troops. Textbook]. Voennoe izdatel'stvo, Moskva, 1982g.

55. Doklad Glavnomu Voennomu Sovetu Krasnoj Armii o novyh sredstvah bor'by v sovremennoj vojne po avtobronetankovomu i protivotankovomu vooruzheniju, 20 maja 1941 goda [Report to the Main Military Council of the Red Army on new means of struggle in modern warfare for armoured and anti-tank weapons, 20 May 1941]. TsAMO, F. 38, O. 11353, D. 895, LL. 22–4.

56. Cirlin, A.D. i dr. Inzhenernye vojska v bojah za Sovetskuju Rodinu [Engineering troops in the battles for the Soviet Motherland]. M.: Voenizdat, 1970, s. 424.

57. Otchet po inzhenernomu obespecheniju 5 Ud. A v Berlinskoj operacii, 09.06.1945 g [Report on engineering support of 5th Shock Army in the Berlin operation, 9 June 1945]. TsAMO, F. 333, O. 4885, D. 339, LL. 629–34.

58. Otchet po inzhenernomu obespecheniju nastupatel'noj operacii po osvobozhdeniju Man'chzhurii, 14.09.1945 g [Report on the engineering support of the offensive operation for the liberation of Manchuria, 14 September 1945]. TsAMO, F. 394, O. 0009095, D. 0059, LL. 269–75 s ob.

59. Kratkij doklad ob inzhenernom obespechenii nastupatel'nyh operacij vojsk 6 gv. TA po osvobozhdeniju Manchzhurii, 23.08.1945 g [A short report on the engineering support of the offensive operations of the 6th Guards TA for the liberation of Manchuria, 23 August 1945]. TsAMO, F. 339, O. 5179, D. 98, LL. 44–6.

60. Soljankin, A.G., Pavlov, M.V., Pavlov, I.V., Zheltov, I.T. Tom 2. Otechestvennye bronirovannye mashiny. 1941–1945 gg. [Domestic Armoured Vehicles, vol. 2, 1941–1945.] M.: OOO Izdatel'skij centr 'Eksprint', 2005, 448 s.: il.

61. Opisanie boevyh dejstvij 8 mehkorpusa s 22.6 po 29.6.1941 g., 18.07.1941 g [Description of the actions of the 8th Mechanized Corps from 22 June to 29 June 1941]. TsAMO, F. 38, O. 11360, D. 2, LL. 105–6.

62. Spravka o sostojanii razvedyvatel'nyh batal'onov 2 TA, 28.02.1944 g [Information about the state of the reconnaissance battalions of the 2nd TA, 28 February 1944]. TsAMO, F. 307, O. 4148, D. 245, LL. 144–5.

63. Vedomost' boevogo sostava vojsk 2 TA, 16.02.1944 g [Bulletin of the combat strength of the troops of the 2nd TA, 16 February 1944]. TsAMO, F. 307, O. 4148, D. 245, L. 119.

64. Svedenija o nekomplekte serzhantskogo i rjadovogo sostava v soedinenijah 2 TA, 26.02.1944 g [Information about the shortage of sergeants and privates in 2 Tank Army, 2 February 1944]. TsAMO, F. 307, O. 4148, D. 245, L. 133.

65. Otchet o rabote Nauchno-Ispitateljnogo Bronetankovogo Poligona GBTU KA za godi velikoj otechestvennoi voyni. 1946 g [Report on the work of the GBTU research test proving grounds for armoured equipment during the years of the Great Patriotic War, 1946]. TsAMO, F. 38, O. 11355a, D. 209b, L. 195.